Academic Articles on Education

By

Brenda Diann Johnson

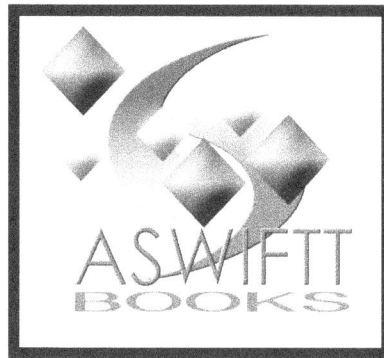

ASWIFTT ENTERPRISES, LLC
Duncanville, Texas 75138

Brenda Diann Johnson
brendadiannjohnson@yahoo.com

Published by
ASWIFTT ENTERPRISES, LLC
Imprint: ASWIFTT BOOKS
P.O. Box 380669
Duncanville, Texas 75138

ISBN: 979-8-9901107-6-2

Library of Congress Control Number: 2024926309

Printed in the United States of America.

Cover Design and Editing by Brenda Diann Johnson
Cover Photo © Maksym Yemelyanov

Dedications

Academic Articles on Education is dedicated to all teachers who educate the masses to inspire, encourage, motivate, enlighten, and correct to move the masses forward.

Acknowledgments

I acknowledge an Almighty God who gave me the passion, creativity, ideas, and inventions to educate the masses. I am determined to be a good steward.

Foreword

_____

"Make a Difference……Teach?"

When I read the motto, "Make a Difference……Teach?" I immediately see a question proposed by the motto. When I look at the motto more closely, I notice that it is two-fold. It makes a bold statement to make a difference, and it proposes a question to the reader.

First, the motto is meant to encourage and boldly challenge the reader to make a difference in the world. Second, the motto proposes the question, Teach? Is teaching the answer to making a difference in the world?

I believe the statement and question proposed in the motto is thought provoking. In fact, in order to make a difference in the world, we must continue to educate. We specifically need to educate those who have influence and those who will have influence on how our nation operates.

Those who have influence on our nation today are our federal, state, and city leaders. These leaders run our nation. They have been trained and educated by teachers in the past to help validate their job credentials.

We rely on our leaders to do a good job and to be knowledgeable in making the right decisions for the country.

It is in the best interest of the nation for our leaders to continue educating themselves throughout their careers. Many enroll in continuing education courses to gain new knowledge and to stay up to date on current issues. Some leaders rely on advisors to help them stay abreast of current issues and new information. In our formal educational institutions, teachers will always play a role in educating those who lead our nation. Informal education is also a benefit. Leaders must do their own research and personal study to make educated decisions when it comes to our nation.

Teachers help shape our nation by educating and preparing our children for the future. Our children are educated in our public and private school systems. They will also be educated in our formal educational institutions beyond high school.

In order for our children to make a difference in our nation, they need to be educated and prepared by individuals, who will boldly accept the challenge.

Teachers are responsible for staying up to date in subjects like Science and Technology, History, Mathematics, Social Sciences, Language Arts, and other subjects as well. Knowledge imparted to children through good teachers will have a positive and powerful impact on our nation in the future.

Teachers not only play a role in formally educating our children, but they also educate our children informally. Teachers have a lot to do with shaping our children's attitudes and beliefs about our nation and the society we live in. From Pre-K through college, attitudes and beliefs are being shaped.

Teachers educate and train children about our nation's past mistakes, present, and mistakes that will be made if the same actions are repeated. Teachers help children analyze and think through problems. They also help encourage children to come up with solutions to problems. Teachers are valuable to our nation. It is because of teachers that our children will know how to fully play out their future roles in society.

Brenda Diann Johnson

Table of Contents

Article 1

Setting the Stage for Multicultural Education in the Classroom

Did you know that you are a STAR? You made it through the auditions and beat others for the part. Your contract is signed and rehearsals are next to prepare you for your initial appearance on set. All eyes will be focused on the classroom stage while anticipating your strategic delivery of the material and objectives you gave. Your students are the audience who make up the crowd to decide if your performance was academically sound.

When teachers enter the classroom at the beginning of a new year they are faced with providing a curriculum that offers equality for all students. According to the Declaration of Independence all men are created equal and they should have the right to life, liberty and the pursuit of happiness. Throughout the nation's history since 1776, marginalized and excluded groups such as women, African Americans, Native Americans, and other cultural and ethnic groups have used this idea to justify and defend the extension of human rights to them and to end institutional discrimination, such as sexism, racism, and discrimination against people with disabilities. (Branch, 2006).

Teachers are also challenged in using teaching strategies to reach each student while incorporating multicultural education. Students come to the classroom with certain philosophies they were taught at home. Students receive their views of the world from their parents. Some students are taught that individual success is very important. They are also taught they can achieve success through hard work. The nuclear family reinforces individualism in U.S. culture. One result of this strong individualism is that married children usually expect their older parents to live independently or in homes for senior citizens rather than with them. The strong individualism in U.S. culture contrasts sharply with the groupism and group commitment found in Asian nations, such as China and Japan. (Butterfield, 1982; Reischauer, 1981).

The teacher also has to decipher between students whose families believe that success lies in their group commitment. People belong to and live in social groups (Bullivant, 1993). A group is a collectivity of persons who share an identity, a feeling of unity. A group is also a social system that has a social structure of interrelated roles (Theodorson & Theodorson, 1969). The group's program for survival, values, ideations, and shared symbols constitutes its culture (Kuper, 1999). Sociologists also assume that knowledge about groups to which an individual belongs provides important clues to and explanations for the individual's behavior. Goodman and Marx (1982) write, "Such factors as shared religion, nationality, age, sex, marital status, and education have proved to be important determinants of what people believe, feel, and do" (p. 7).

When teachers get to know their students at the beginning of the year they can effectively create curriculums that incorporate multicultural education. According to Banks, multicultural education has five dimensions. Establishing a multicultural education curriculum is not enough to achieve multicultural education in the classroom. He further states "Multicultural education is also a reform movement designed to bring about a transformation of the school so that students from both genders and from diverse cultural, language, and ethnic groups will have an equal chance to experience school success."

The five dimensions of multicultural education are content integration, knowledge construction, equity pedagogy, prejudice reduction and empowering school culture.

When teachers prepare their lesson plans throughout the school year they must incorporate all five multicultural education dimensions. Content integration is where teachers start when gathering the material they want to teach. In this stage teachers must be careful to find material from all cultures to make up the material content for their lesson. They should also have visual examples from various cultures. Having examples from various cultures will play a key part with visual, auditory and kinesthetic learners. Knowledge construction is also important when teachers plan their lessons. It is the teacher's job to help students understand, investigate, and determine how the implicit cultural assumptions, frames of reference, perspectives and biases within a discipline influence the ways in which knowledge is constructed. (Banks, 2009) Planned problem solving activities and applying who, what, when, where and why questions are great tools to use to help students understand the content of the lesson.

Equity pedagogy must also be included when teachers do their lesson plans. When teachers apply this dimension they modify their teaching strategies to help students from all diverse racial, gender, cultural and social-class groups achieve academic success. When teachers are choosing content material and strategies for lesson plans they are mindful of student prejudices. It is the teacher's job to reduce racial prejudices in the classroom. This can be done when teachers choose content material from various cultures while highlighting the positive values from each culture. The last dimension of multicultural education is empowering school culture. With this dimension the ratio of student achievement from different cultural backgrounds must be reflected equally in labeling, grouping and sports participation in the schools. Students must also have equal interaction with staff across racial and ethnic lines to create a school culture that empowers students from various racial, ethnic and gender groups.

When teachers carefully craft their lesson plans they must also choose a method of delivery that also projects multicultural education. Teachers use different teaching approaches to help students master the content taught in class. Teaching approaches include the Multicultural Approach, the Single Group Approach, the Human Relations Approach and the Multicultural Social Justice Approach. It is up to teachers to choose the best teaching approach for the students they teach.

Teachers tend to gather information on students at the beginning of the year by using activities to collect such data. Activities for K to 12 can range from family projects, student collages, emergency contact information, first day introductions, or all about me projects. These activities give information to help teachers plan curriculums that reflect their students.

Choosing a teaching approach becomes easy when teachers know their class makeup. The teaching approach is also based on the objective of the lesson taught.

Teachers who choose the Human Relations Approach have the objective to help students learn to live together harmoniously in a world that is becoming smaller and smaller and they believe that greater social equality will result if students learn to respect one another regardless of race, class, gender, or disability. (Banks, 2013, p. 47)

The curriculum for the human relations approach addresses individual differences and similarities. Teachers also use cooperative learning, role-playing, and vicarious or real experiences to help the students develop appreciation of others. (Banks, 2013, p. 47)

Some teachers use the Single Group Approach to raise the social status of the target group by helping young people examine how the group has been oppressed historically despite its capabilities and achievements. It focuses on one specific group at a time so the history, perspectives, and worldview of that group can be developed coherently rather than piecemeal. It also examines the current social status of the group and actions taken historically as well as contemporarily to further the group's interests. Single-group studies are oriented toward political action and liberation. Advocates of this approach hope that students will develop more respect for the group as well as the knowledge and commitment needed to work to improve the group's status in society. (Banks, 2013, p. 48)

The Multicultural Social Justice Approach is chosen by teachers who want students to experience democracy. They help students put democracy into action through learning how the three branches of government work. Students practice politics, debates, social action and the use of power. (Osler & Starkey, 2005)

With the Multicultural Social Justice Approach students also learn how to recognize institutional inequality, how to take social action and how to work together with other oppressed groups. (Banks, 2013, p. 51)

It is also important to have a teaching strategy that works for you. Your daily goal is to deliver an excellent presentation on the classroom stage. As a teacher I always start with examining the Texas Essentials Knowledge and Skills (TEKS) which are the teaching objectives designed for each grade level. (http://www.tea.state.tx.us) I choose the objectives that I want to teach for the week, month, or semester. When I have gathered the TEKS, I choose a lesson model or presentation method to help students master the objective. I decide what outcome I want for my class while focusing on the content presented.

When I am choosing the content taught I also choose the props, worksheets, and student activities that best demonstrate the objective of the lesson. I also use computer resources and other technology to help visual, auditory and kinesthetic learners. After the content is chosen for the lesson I also decide on the assessment

method to evaluate students' mastery of the material. The test results will give

feedback that teachers need to prepare for future lessons.

References

Branch, T. (2006). *At Canaan's edge: America in the King years, 1965–68*. New York: Simon & Schuster.

Butterfield, F. (1982). *China: Alive in the bitter sea*. New York: Bantam.

Reischauer, E. O. (1981). *The Japanese*. Cambridge, MA: Harvard University Press.

Bullivant, B. (1993). Culture: Its nature and meaning for educators. In J. A. Banks & C. A. M. Banks (Eds.), *Multicultural education: Issues and perspectives* (2nd ed., pp. 29–47). Boston: Allyn & Bacon.

Theodorson, G. A., & Theodorson, A. G. (1969). *A modern dictionary of sociology*. New York: Barnes & Noble.

Kuper, A. (1999). *Culture: The anthropologists' account*. Cambridge, MA: Harvard University Press.

Goodman, N., & Marx, G. T. (1982). *Society today* (4th Ed.). New York: Random House.

Banks, J. A. (Ed.). (2009). *The Routledge international companion to multicultural education*. New York and London: Routledge.

Banks, J. A., & McGhee Banks, C. A. (Eds.). (2013). *Multicultural Education: Issues and Perspectives (8th Ed.)*. Hoboken, NJ: John Wiley & Sons.

Osler, A., & Starkey, H. (2005). *Changing citizenship: Democracy and inclusion in education*. New York: McGraw-Hill Education

(http://www.tea.state.tx.us)

Article 2

Modeling Multicultural Education

Immigration continues to be the issue in our United States public school systems. Immigrants give rise to the largest part of linguistic diversity among students and are also the fastest-growing group of students in U.S. schools (Oh & Cooc, 2011). In fact, almost all the growth in the child population of the United States in the last two decades can be accounted for by children of immigrants (Cervantes & Hernandez, 2011; Fortuny, Hernandez, & Chaudry, 2010).

Many demographers predict that by 2025, approximately 20 to 25 percent of immigrant students enrolled in public schools will have limited proficiency in English (Spellings, 2005). Because the growth of diverse students in public schools continue to increase it is imperative that teachers provide a multicultural education for students. Teachers also need to create curriculums that reflect the diverse student population in their classrooms.

Teachers can help students by using the interactionist theory when providing a multicultural education for all students. The *Interactionist theory* (Lightbown & Spada, 2006) has widely influenced and been influenced by research on and teaching in immersion programs in Canada. The basic tenet of this theory is that both input and output are crucial for language learning. Teachers who draw on this theory create tasks for which conversational interactions between speakers are central to the process of language learning.

Multicultural Education has become the focus in our schools today. It is very important to provide quality education for children of all races. Teachers have used curriculum approaches such as contribution, additive, transformation and social action to include unique information in their lesson plans. These approaches have been effective as direct instruction. Students are taught how to work together with the opposite gender, other races, ethnicities, and those who have different sexual orientations. Multicultural Education in the classroom is a valuable asset to students. It is also equally important to allow students to use the information they learn in real life situations.

Students can put into practice what they have learned at a local Wal-Mart Super Center where diverse people come together. Wal-Mart is a place that provides interaction of cultures, races, genders and groups. Students will be taken to three different departments in the store. In this project students will be taken to the grocery section, the electronics department and the self check-out line.   Students

will see the interactions of people of different genders, races, cultures, and sexual

orientations.

This project can also be enacted in a classroom setting with props such as empty

cereal boxes, waffle boxes, egg cartons, crackers, popcorn, pizza boxes, pop tarts,

TV dinner boxes, etc. Students will also bring unopened can goods such as green

beans, corn, peaches, greens, peas, carrots, etc. Diverse students and students

playing roles of diverse customers will be needed in the classroom project.

The assessment for this project is performance based. Students will be graded

by a rubric and will be given peer feedback from surveys students fill out. This

project will deal with 3 scenarios dealing with gender, sexual orientation, and

ethnicity. The method of handling these implications are dealt with in the 3

performance scenarios.

The objective of the field trip is to allow students to use their social, creative,

analytical, and problem-solving skills. Students will also use the information they

learned about multicultural education in the classroom. Three different scenario

environments will be used to test students' knowledge mastery of multicultural

education.

Students will witness a real-life scenario dealing with sexual orientation. It is important that students learn how to respond to others who have chosen an alternative lifestyle. These individuals are members of our communities. Students must learn they will also work on jobs with individuals who are members of the Gay, Lesbian, Bisexual, Transgender and Queer (GLBTQ) community.

Many people use their religion as the reason to be bigoted toward those who are different. Regardless of religious beliefs, the reality is that GLBT's are in the workplace and in the marketplace. Each time prejudice is tolerated the business runs the risk of litigation, lost business, and a lost opportunity to attract and retain the best talent for the job, regardless of sexual orientation. (http://www.sideroad.com/Diversity_in_the_Workplace/sexual-orientation-in-the-workplace.html)

Neither the government nor businesses expect workers to change their beliefs or values as it relates to sexual orientation or any other difference among people at work. However, it is expected that all employees will be held accountable for their own behavior. When GLBT (gay, lesbian, bisexual and transgendered) jokes, gestures, and rumors are tolerated at work, it creates an environment that negatively affects productivity even if there are no GLBT's present. Such behavior can also be offensive to heterosexuals, who are not biased in this way, and many workers who have friends and relatives who are other than heterosexual. (http://www.sideroad.com/Diversity_in_the_Workplace/sexual-orientation-in-the-workplace.html)

In scenario 1, two students will be chosen to interact. One student will play the customer and the other student will be the Wal-Mart employee who has a different sexual orientation. The Wal-Mart employee is assigned to the grocery section. The customer is having problems finding a favorite cereal. The customer has purchased a specific type of cereal before at this particular Wal-Mart but does not see it on the shelf. The only Wal-Mart employee on the cereal aisle is a gay male. His appearance signifies that he has chosen an alternative lifestyle. He is shelving cereal on this aisle. Keep in mind there is no one else to assist the customer on this aisle but the gay male. The teacher will grade the student on mannerisms, body language, tone, language, word usage, eye contact, volume in voice, facial expressions and acceptance or inclusion during the interaction.

The teacher will also look to see if the student playing the customer is focused on finding the cereal and receiving the help the store employee offers to give and not focus on the person's sexual orientation or mannerisms.

Students must also learn how to respect each other when it comes to males and females. Gender should never be a factor when applying for jobs. People should be judged on their qualifications, talents and credentials for the job they desire.

Gender bias begins as early as elementary school education--long before entering the workforce. Citing research conducted by I. Weiss in the late 1980s, Carolyn Butcher Dickman, the author of "Gender Differences and Instructional Discrimination in the Classroom," writes, "Most K through 8 teachers, almost all women, suffer from inadequate preparation in science so that they fear teaching science and lack confidence in their ability to do so." Consequently, according to Dickman, "The quality of teacher contacts varies between the genders. Boys receive more teacher reactions of praise, criticism and remediation." (http://smallbusiness.chron.com/implications-gender-bias-workplace-2865.html)

Gender bias occurs because of personal values, perceptions and outdated, traditional views about men and women. When the topic of gender bias comes up, it's usually within the context of women being victims of workplace discrimination. There are social and financial implications of gender bias in the workforce. Understanding the implications of gender bias, along with diversity training and exposure to a significant percentage of women in the workforce, can minimize the incidents of unfair employment practices.

(http://smallbusiness.chron.com/implications-gender-bias-workplace-2865.html)

Scenario 2 will take place in the electronics department. Students can bring their favorite electronic toy or gadget to set up in a classroom scene. In this scene a female and male student will be chosen. The female will be the Wal-Mart employee who works in the electronics department. The male will be the customer who is shopping for a tablet to update his company information while he is on a business trip. The only person he sees in the electronics department is a female. The teacher will judge the male and female interaction when discussing computers. The teacher will look for facial expressions, mannerisms, body language, tone, volume, and language, choice of words, and confidence in both the male and female while carrying out their roles. It is known that males are perceived to have more knowledge about technology and science. In this scenario the male will have to prove that he can be helped with his computer purchase by a female who educates him about the technology of the tablet he purchases.

In this scenario the teacher will look for the female's self-confidence to deliver information on the tablet to educate the customer. The female employee does not need to focus on the fact that the customer is a male. Her job is to deliver excellent customer service regardless of the gender. The teacher will also look for the male's perception of the female. The male customer's job is to show respect to the Wal-Mart employee regardless of gender. The Wal-Mart electronics employee is considered the expert in this department and the male customer should treat the employee with respect.

The last scenario will deal with race, culture and ethnicity. With the ongoing increase in immigration students will continue to see diverse students in the classroom. Students must learn to work together with other cultures because they will see different races, cultures and ethnicities in their future jobs.

Most people would agree that cultural diversity in the workplace utilizes our country's skills to its fullest and contributes to our overall growth and prosperity. The reality of the situation is that it hasn't happened, and progress remains slow. While we are in the midst of the longest period of economic growth this country has ever seen, the gap between the "haves" and "have nots" continues to widen. (http://www.ethnicmajority.com/corporate_diversity.htm)

One of the reasons for this has been the lack of diversity in corporate America. By not developing a diverse workforce from the top down, African, Hispanic (Latino), and Asian Americans are unfairly relegated to lower-skilled, lower-pay positions and are not able to fulfill their true potential. Many corporations have recognized that diversity contributes to the bottom line by: making it easier to retain good <u>employees</u>, lowering costs by developing skills in-house, and developing a reputation that helps attract new employees. This is especially important with the economy doing so well, and the demand for skilled labor at record levels. (http://www.ethnicmajority.com/corporate_diversity.htm)

Scenario 3 will take place in the self-check-out line. The props needed for the classroom scene are a cash register, scanner, desk to place groceries, plastic bags for groceries, store clerk who manages the self-check-out line, and 6 people who are standing in line to check out. In this scenario there will be many different races in line to check out. Two students will be chosen to act out this scene. There will be a student of Anglo-American decent and a student who is from Tanzania with a thick accent. The Anglo-American student will be challenged to help the customer from Tanzania when he asks for help in operating the scanner and the whole process of the self check-out line. The teacher will look for facial expressions, mannerisms, body language, tone, volume, language, choice of words, and the willingness to help even though the Anglo-American customer has problems with the Tanzanian male's accent.

The teacher will also look for the Anglo-American male's willingness to help regardless of the other customer's culture, race or ethnicity. The Anglo-American male will use modeling if he and the Tanzanian male do not understand each other.

Modeling the self-check-out process does not require talking.

The students who are observing and not participating directly in each scene will be responsible for filling out a survey as each scene is enacted. On the survey the students will give points from 1 to 10 in each category of facial expressions, mannerisms, body language, tone, volume, language, choice of words, and the willingness to help. These surveys will be given to each student as peer feedback. Each student will have their turn to participate in at least one scenario and will receive a grade from the teacher and peer feedback.

The assessment the teacher will use is a performance assessment method. Students will apply what they learned in class about multicultural education and how to interact with different groups in society. Students will also use problem solving skills, originality, and they will justify each action they choose to use in their performance. Peer feedback and teacher evaluations will also give student feedback on whether each student's justification was appropriate for the situation they were given.

When teachers allow students to experience real life situations it enhances their education. Teachers should use every resource to model learning strategies. When teachers use modeling strategies it helps students master the material. Real life experiences create opportunities that allow students to have fun while learning new things.

References

Cervantes, W. D., & Hernandez, D. J. (2011, March). Children in immigrant families: Ensuring opportunity for every child in America. *First Focus and Foundation for Child Development.*

http://www.firstfocus.net/sites/default/files/FCDimmigration.pdf.

Fortuny, K., Hernandez, D. J., & Chaudry, A. (2010). *Young children of immigrants: The leading edge of America's future.* Washington, DC: Urban Institute.

Lightbown, P., & Spada, N. (2006). *How languages are learned* (3rd ed.). New York: Oxford University Press.

Oh, S. S., & Cooc, N. (2011). Immigration, youth and education: Editors' introduction. *Harvard Educational Review, 8I(3),* 396-406.

Spellings, M. (2005). *Academic gains of English language learners prove high standards, accountability paying off* Retrieved from http://www.ed.gov/news/speeches/2005/12/l 2012005.html.

http://www.sideroad.com/Diversity_in_the_Workplace/sexual-orientation-in-the-workplace.html

http://smallbusiness.chron.com/implications-gender-bias-workplace-2865.html

http://www.ethnicmajority.com/corporate_diversity.htm

Article 3

A Diversified ToolBOX

It is always wise for teachers to have various resources in their toolbox. Educators will encounter many teaching situations every day because all students are unique. Students also have different learning styles such as visual, auditory and kinesthetic. I currently utilize my teaching and training skills to educate adults. I train adults in writing, leadership & development, and insurance licensing classes. In the writing classes I also utilize my English, Language Arts and Reading (ELAR) skills to help adults who want to learn the mechanics of writing, who are studying to get their GED or who just want to improve their writing skills.

Creating A Multicultural Curriculum

Creativity is very important when preparing a multicultural curriculum. Teachers must take into account the demographics of their classroom. The demographics of a classroom include race, age, sex, culture, special needs, economic status, English language learners, etc. When these variables are taken into consideration the teacher can plan the lesson activities accordingly. One misconception that some teachers may have is that English language learners only include those who come from Mexico and speak Spanish. English language learners can also include students from other countries who speak other languages.

When teachers embrace knowledge instead of misconceptions it empowers them to be more culturally responsive.

Culturally Responsive Self-Directed Learning

In a culturally diverse classroom teachers will serve as mediators in modifying classroom dialogue for self-directed instruction. Educators mediate dialogue with their students on the spot. They adjust the dialogue to extend or refocus a student's response to move him or her to the next rung on the learning ladder. Teachers also use mental modeling which is the active demonstration of strategies by which students can better learn and retain the content taught. These strategies have been applied in the culturally diverse classroom through various forms of social interaction to encourage students to construct their own meanings and interpretations and to revise and extend them under the guidance of the teacher. (Borich, 2011)

Skills as Culturally Responsive Teacher

In the past I remember utilizing my Spanish speaking skills when I taught Pre-Kindergarten. I took Spanish two years in high school and in college I took Spanish four years. Little did I know that my investment in learning the language of Spanish would benefit my teaching career years later. I remember a little girl who came to my Pre-Kindergarten class who would not talk in class. She seemed to understand the lesson activities from watching her peers at the table where she sat. I wanted to reach out more to this student because she was a foster child who had already been enrolled in several schools. She was behind in her academics because she never stayed at a school long enough to complete a school year.

My new student also had other siblings who attended the same school in different grades. All the teachers who taught these children were briefed by the administration about their situation. I decided to work with my students one on one during recess and after whole group sessions in class. I also decided to speak Spanish to my student when I was unsure if she understood what I was saying in English. Unfortunately, we did not get a chance to finish the special curriculum I prepared. Once again, the student and her siblings were unenrolled out of school. I was disappointed when I found out she was unenrolled from my class. I still think about this student today. As a teacher I wanted to help and make an impact on her life.

My Professional Skills and Areas of Improvement

Today, I continue to work on being a culturally responsive teacher for both children and adults. I utilize every skill that God has blessed me to obtain. I am proficient in reading and writing in both English and Spanish. I enjoyed learning the language of Spanish just as much as I enjoy the English language. The area I want to improve is speaking Spanish fluently. I believe this area can be mastered

when I seek out the right class and resources to accomplish it. I also want to

publish more children's books in Spanish. I currently have a children's book titled

"My Baby Sister" which is available in both English and Spanish. (Johnson, 2013)

References

Borich, G. (2011). The Effective Teacher. In *Effective teaching methods: Research-based practice* (7th ed.). Boston, MA: Pearson Education.

Johnson, B. (2013). *My Baby Sister*. Duncanville, TX: ASWIFTT Publishing, LLC.

Article 4

An Excellent Classroom Environment

Every year teachers have the responsibility of decorating the room they will conduct their classes. Teachers must be creative and think outside the box to make their rooms enticing to students. They must also come up with ideas that inspire students to learn and resolve problems independently. Classrooms should make students feel welcomed and secure. Students should also love their learning environment.

If money were no object and I was the recipient of an educational grant from Microsoft I would invest in my classroom. There are five categories that need to be fulfilled to have an excellent classroom environment. The five categories are curriculum, environment, books, resources and technology. Teachers need to have support from administration to accomplish their goals for the classroom. It is imperative for administration, teachers, students and parents to work in concert for students to have academic success.

Curriculum

Teachers are responsible for setting the stage early for students to excel during the year. For students to achieve academic success they must have a solid curriculum. Teachers must begin by aligning their lesson plans to their state curriculum standards. In the state of Texas, the state curriculum is called the Texas Essentials Knowledge and Skills (TEKS). Grade levels K to 12 have specific TEKS for each grade level and each core subject. These TEKS must be taught each year before students take state mandated tests at the end of the year. Teachers should also align their lesson plans with the demographics of their classroom. Incorporating diversity is a key factor in today's classroom setting. (http://tea.texas.gov/curriculum/teks)

The instructional approaches that would be used are direct and indirect instruction and problem-based learning. Direct instruction would consist of lectures that are given by the teacher. The lecture material is information that students will see on assessments. Indirect instruction would consist of probing questions to check for student understanding after each topic in the lecture. In problem based learning the teacher adopts the role as facilitator while guiding students through the learning process. Students become investigators and problem solvers to an open-ended question they are given. Assessments would also be varied. Tests would include presentations, oral and written tests, projects and research papers. (http://www.learning-theories.com/problem-based-learning-pbl.html)

Environment

The second category is to invest in the classroom environment. Teachers should not have to decorate classrooms every year and then take down decorations at the end of the year. I would take the lead by recommending that the school district invest in permanent decorations for each classroom. There would be colorful illustrations on the walls of each classroom. Each classroom would have a core subject theme that would educate students with pictures. The colorful illustrations would specifically pertain to the subject being taught. All math classrooms would have pictures of everything that dealt with Math, in English, Language Arts, and Literature the classrooms would have illustrations that only pertained to ELAR, in Science classrooms the illustrations on the wall would only pertain to Science, in Social Studies and History classrooms the illustrations would only pertain to Social Studies and History. In all electives the illustrations would only pertain to that elective.

I believe that students enjoy coming to a colorful classroom no matter what age or grade level. The colorful pictures and illustrations on classroom walls are alternative ways to educate students. Students are learning when they see pictures that represent meaningful information. Pictures and illustrations benefit all learners such as visual, auditory, and kinesthetic. Teachers can use pictures and illustrations to demonstrate and give examples in class lectures.

Books

The third category that I would invest in are books. It is very important for students to have updated books. When schools have outdated books, teachers must supplement their lesson plans with alternative resources. Students also deserve the best resources available on the market. Teachers should do their research to invest in books that have been evaluated by other professional educators. Books that have the most useful and effective information should be chosen as a resource for classrooms. They should also be evaluated to see if they include information that promotes multiculturalism.

Resources & Technology

The fourth category that I would invest in is resources. Having the right resources in a classroom makes a world of difference. Resources include alternative lecture materials, books, schools supply for students, paper, art supplies, library books, copy paper, testing materials, resources for student centers, and the list goes on and on. I would also have an area for circle time. This area would include a large colorful rug for students to sit on, a rocking chair for the storyteller which would be a parent or community volunteer. Parents and community volunteers would also be needed to donate supplies, resources, and snacks year around. I would also have throw pillows on the floor and bookshelves full of books for the classroom library. There would be full hands-on operational centers for younger ages and older students would have center boxes they could carry back to their desks.

The last category is technology. My desire is for each student to have an assigned computer in the classroom. Each computer will also have internet and intranet capabilities. Students need access to a desktop computer to help them with their classwork and research assignments. Some students do not have computers at home, so they need access to one at school. Other classroom technology would include tablets for each student, a laptop for the teacher, a projector, whiteboard, and podium for teacher and student presentations.

References

http://tea.texas.gov/curriculum/teks

http://www.learning-theories.com/problem-based-learning-pbl.html

Article 5

Personal Learning Theory

Abstract

Educating students should be the priority of all teachers. Students rely on professional educators to prepare them for their future. When teachers enter the field of education they should adopt the belief that all students are teachable. They must also eliminate all biases in their planned curriculum. They should also plan lesson activities for all students and their learning styles. It is important to create allies with parents. Teachers should communicate with parents about grades, student progress, and student support services. Planning for student success overall involves using a multicultural curriculum, creating lesson plans for all learning styles, and re-teaching when necessary.

Target Audience

The target audience for my learning theory are six graders who are 12 years old. These students are from all cultures and backgrounds such as African, Latino, Asian and Anglo American students. This target audience are students from the "Intro to Media" class. They are looking forward to learning about each genre in Media such as newspaper, radio, television, books, magazines, speech and debate.

Theories That Apply To Target Audience

The two theories that apply to 6th grade students are Situated Learning and The Constructivist Theory. J. Lave argues that learning as it normally occurs is a function of the activity, context and culture in which it occurs as situated. This contrasts with most classroom learning activities which involve knowledge which is abstract and out of context. Social interaction is a critical component of situated learning. Students become involved in a "community of practice" which embodies certain beliefs and behaviors to be acquired. As the beginner or newcomer moves from the periphery of this community to its center, they become more active and engaged within the culture and hence assume the role of expert or old-timer. Furthermore, situated learning is usually unintentional rather than deliberate. (http://www.instructionaldesign.org/theories/situated-learning.html)

In the Constructivist Theory, A major theme in the theoretical framework of Bruner is that learning is an active process in which learners construct new ideas or concepts based upon their current or past knowledge. The learner selects and transforms information, constructs hypotheses, and makes decisions, relying on a cognitive structure to do so. Cognitive structure or mental models provides meaning and organization to experiences and allows the individual to "go beyond the information given". A constructivist teacher encourages students to construct their own knowledge and a flipped classroom shifts instruction out of the classroom and assignments into the classroom. You can use flipped learning for students to learn the basic concepts before coming to class so that you can use class time for students to explore the concepts in depth and to construct their own knowledge. (Chang, 2016)

When students discover principles by themselves, they can construct their own knowledge. Educators and students should engage in an active dialog which is socratic learning. The task of the instructor is to translate information to be learned into a format appropriate to the learner's current state of understanding. Curriculum should be organized in a spiral manner so that the student continually builds upon what they have already learned. (http://www.instructionaldesign.org/theories/constructivist.html)

Aspects of My Theory

The aspects of my learning theory include planning a detailed curriculum while considering the demographics of my classroom. Even though students attend the same class, listen to the same lecture, participate in the same classroom activities, read the same book, they may have a different understanding of the same topic. It is because students do not come to class as blank slates, but as learners with prior experience on the topic. When they encounter new experiences, they incorporate it with their prior experiences to produce a unique understanding of the topic.

(Chang, 2016) Learning styles such as auditory, visual and kinesthetic will also be

considered. Students learn best when teachers model the learning objectives. The

learning objectives for six graders are taken from the Texas state curriculum. The

state curriculum is what students will be tested on at the end of the school year.

The writing objectives are taught in my course "Intro to Media." Students master

the learning objectives when they do hands on activities. Project based learning

gives students the opportunity to put into practice what they learned from the class

lectures in each unit. Students are also taken on field trips so they can experience

the environment of a newsroom at a radio or television station.

Strategy For Using Personal Learning Theory

The strategy I will use to reach the six grade population in "Intro to Media" is

first create a curriculum that includes the Texas Essentials Knowledge and Skills

for English, Language Arts and Reading for six grade. The objectives will be

incorporated in each class activity. Students will also be tested for mastery over

each objective. Tests include oral, written, and performance assessments.

Students will be responsible for showing mastery of objectives. Students will also

be re-taught if they failed to master the lesson objectives. Project based learning

will be utilized to help students grasp the lesson content. Independent study has

also proved to be benefitual. Online guest speakers have proven to be a highly effective and credible method aimed at reinforcing course concepts, and add

breadth to course learning examples and activities within pedagogical events

(Eveleth & Eveleth, 2009)

Student Success Learning Theory

In order for students to succeed in their academic career they must have

educators who care. These educators must also create curriculums that match the

demographics of their classroom. They must be willing to teach and take all biases

out of the content material. Teachers must incorporate all learning styles such as

auditory, visual and kinesthetic. They must also believe all students are teachable.

It is important to create allies with parents to provide the best academic plan for

students.

References

Eveleth, D. M., & Baker-Eveleth, L. J. 2009. Student Dialogue with Online Guest Speakers. Decision Sciences Journal of Innovative Education, 7 (2), 417-421.

Chang, S. (2016). The Marriage of Constructivism and Flipped Learning. Retrieved December 7, 2016, from: http://www.eric.ed.gov/contentdelivery/servlet/ERICServlet?accno=ED565608

Li, L., & Guo, R. (2015). A Student-Centered Guest Lecturing: A Constructivism Approach to Promote Student Engagement. Retrieved December 8, 2016, from http://www.eric.ed.gov/contentdelivery/servlet/ERICServlet?accno=EJ1060070

http://www.instructionaldesign.org/theories/situated-learning.html

http://www.instructionaldesign.org/theories/constructivist.html

Article 6

Let's Get Radical

Scenario:

It is the desire of all parents to offer the best education for their kids. The "Every Student Succeeds Act" signed by President Barack Obama on December 10, 2015 now gives educators more creativity to help students academically. The Every Student Succeeds Act ushers in more flexibility and stability after years of uncertainty about the future of No Child Left Behind. Critics said states would feel less pressure to fix the worst-performing schools. However, educators will continue to be responsible for assessing their students. States must test students yearly in reading and math in grades three through eight, and once in high school. The bill will end the federal guidelines for defining school quality and require states to set up their own accountability systems to measure improvement. States will also determine how to intervene in the bottom 5% of schools and those with low graduation rates. States must also show test data for children in different "subgroups" of students, such as racial minorities, students in poverty and English-language learners. Overall, the bill allows states to devise their own ways to address achievement gaps. (Brody, 2015)

For example, Rad Nickels is a 4th grade student who has been identified as at risk. Rad is having problems with reading comprehension, social studies and science. He is also having problems in math from time to time, although it is his favorite subject. Rad and his family were also homeless for a period of 3 years when his father lost his job. The financial set back had a major affect on Rad's grades and attendance. Rad was angry about issues he had at home and took his frustrations out on other students in school. Rad bullied other students for various reasons. Rad's Language Arts teacher also feels that he may have some special needs. Initially, Rad's academic problems were left undetected. He was not given the help he needed in his core subject classes. His grades suffered and a progress report was not sent home to inform his parents before report cards came out. Teachers labeled him as a bad student. They did not investigate further why Rad was having problems in his classes. According to Derrick Meador, an at risk-student can be defined as a student who struggles in an area or several areas. Those struggles often have an adverse affect on the student's performance at school. A student can be deemed an at risk due to several factors including low test scores, poor attendance, discipline issues, structure at home, socioeconomic status, and others. Most schools have programs such as Title I that provide more attention to the students and are designed to keep them from falling through the cracks. (Meador, 2015)

In Texas, Dallas ISD has detailed its criteria for At-Risk students in their State Compensatory Education Program. At-Risk students are grades PK-3 who did not perform satisfactorily on a readiness test during the current school year, grades 7-12 who did not maintain an average equivalent to at least 70 on a scale of 100 in two or more subjects during the semester, a student who was not advanced from one grade level to the next, students who did not perform satisfactorily on an assessment instrument administered under TEC Chapter 30, Sub-chapter B, and has not in the previous or current school year, and a student who is pregnant or is a parent. Students are also at-risk if they have been placed in an alternative education program during the preceding or current school year, have been expelled during the preceding or current school year; are currently on parole, probation, deferred prosecution, or other conditional release, and was previously reported through PEIMS to have dropped out of school. Other at-risk students include students of limited English proficiency (LEP), those who are in custody or care of the Department of Protective and Regulatory Services. Students who are homeless, those who reside in a residential placement facility, detention facility, a substance abuse treatment facility, emergency shelter, psychiatric hospital, halfway house, or foster group home.

(http://www.dallasisd.org/cms/lib/TX01001475/Centricity/domain/98/evaluation/1
1-12/finalrpts/EA11-301-2-SCE-Report-Final.pdf)

Set Behavioral Goals:

Now that we know the criteria for at-risk students mentioned previously, Rad
needs to be identified as at-risk. It is important to set behavioral and academic
goals for him before it's too late. Rad needs to be shown compassion. His teacher
along with the school district needs to create a plan that will address his issues.
The desired behavior for Rad is to improve his grades, decrease absences, improve
reading comprehension, and follow the requirements in his behavioral contract.

1. Identify at-risk students immediately by the criteria set by the district.
2. Match student up with appropriate student services available in the school,
   district and community
3. Establish a solid teacher/parent relationship. Make sure parents are allies with
   the teacher to help Rad improve behavior and academics.
4. Teach state curriculum objectives for all core subjects on Rad's academic level.
5. Use the reading resources set forth in the Literacy Education Program for the
   district to improve reading comprehension.
6. Set up a Behavior Contract with teacher, student and parent.

The behavioral goals were set to get Rad the help he needs. The first thing that needs to happen is for Rad to be identified as at-risk. He also needs to be tested for any special needs. Once Rad is identified as at-risk he can qualify to get help from student support services offered by the school district. Rad's parents need to have a strong presence in his education. They should also help his teacher reinforce good behavior. The behavior contract must include the teacher, student and parents' signature.

Determine Appropriate Reinforcers:

When making a decision to use reinforcers, teachers must choose based on the individual needs of the student. Positive reinforcement refers to the presentation of a reinforcer (satisfying stimulus) contingent upon a response that results in the strengthening of that response. On the other hand, negative reinforcement strengthens a response through the removal of an aversive stimulus contingent upon that response. (Driscoll, 2005) One appropriate reinforcer for Rad is giving immediate feedback. Teachers should also write positive notes on his paper for his effort. Rad's assignments that receive a grade B or higher should be displayed with other students outside the class for others to see. Other reinforcers include sending a note home to Rad's parents to comment on the progress in his behavior and academics. Rad's teacher should sit down with him every week to develop a portfolio of his assignments, activities and test scores to share with his parents.

Ludwig and Maehr (1967), for example, demonstrated that making simple statements of approval regarding students' performance in a physical education class led to their making many more positive statements about themselves. Likewise, psychology students discovered that the incidence of seat belt use dramatically increased when grocery store checkers said to customers, "Be sure to buckle up. Remember, [store name] cares about your safety, too." (J. Bailey, personal communication)

The reinforcers used for Rad are specific to his issues. Rad is having problems with some of his core subjects. He has also had problems at home which has spilled over into school. The reinforcers chosen will help Rad gain confidence when given immediate feedback on his assignments. When Rad earns 80% or higher on his assignments they will be displayed among his peers outside the classroom. This will help Rad gain acceptance with his peers who he has also bullied in the past. Rad will receive a whole new outlook when he achieves the behavioral and academic goals set for him by the teacher. Rad's accomplishments is great for the classroom environment, teacher and students.

Select Procedures For Changing Behavior:

In order to change Rad's behavior and academic status a plan must be put in place. The teacher will use strategies that incorporate behaviorism and constructivism. Both behaviorist and constructivist learning theories are impacting practices in schools today. Behaviorists theories undergird the design of many basal textbooks and standardized tests. Also, many special education and behavior management strategies are based on behaviorist theories. At the same time, teachers are implementing many curriculum reforms based on constructivist theories. Cognitive constructivism stems from the later work of Jean Piaget, social-historical constructivism, but they are familiar with elements of constructivist teaching, like building learning communities, understanding children's thinking to scaffold their learning, sharing power with students' to help them solve problems and take responsibility for themselves and others, and assessing students' learning in multiple, authentic ways. A popular, grassroots movement for literacy instruction, called whole language, incorporates all of these characteristics (Kamii, Manning, & Manning, 1991) (Woolley & Woolley, 1999)

To help Rad achieve the behavioral and academic goals a meeting will be scheduled for his parents and teacher to review Rad's behavior contract. The meeting will also be used to discuss the factors that identify Rad as an at-risk student. The meeting will also uncover if Rad needs to be tested for special needs. Rad will receive a folder to document communication between his teacher and parents. The folder will include Rad's daily work, test scores, homework assignments, behavior comments and any important announcements. This folder will help the teacher and parents to monitor Rad's behavior and academic progress. Once it has been determined that Rad is at-risk his teacher and parents will match Rad with the appropriate student support services available in the school district. When Rad gets the student support services that he needs he will excel in areas where he once failed. Rad's teacher will use differentiated instruction to help him master state objectives. The teacher will model the lesson objectives to help students with class assignments and activities. Rad will also receive one on one tutoring before or after school. The tutoring will help Rad stay focused. The tutor will also break down key concepts for Rad so he will understand his class assignments. He will also receive help from the school district literary resources to help him with his reading comprehension.

Implement Procedures and Record Results:

At the conclusion of the meeting with Rad's parents and his teacher the observations of the procedures to help Rad will begin next week. Rad's teacher will prepare a folder for him to take home daily to communicate with his parents. Comments will also be recorded about how things are done in the classroom and at home. The teacher will review Rad's behavior contract each day to see if he is meeting the requirements. So far Rad has followed all classroom directions. He has also been consistent in taking his folder home to communicate his behavior and academic progress in the classroom. Every week Rad's teacher will record if he has taken his folder home. He will also be observed on his test scores and portfolio of his assignments. Rad has also been identified as an at-risk student. Rad can now receive the student support services available to the school distict. With the help of student support services, Rad's grades have improved in reading, social studies, science and math. His overall scores are looking good for the semester. Rad's academic scores were once in the low 40%. Rad now feels confident and can face any challenge. He is no longer a bully. Rad wants to help others along the way.

Evaluate and Revise:

Rad has made significant progress with his behavior and academic goals. At the end of the semester Rad has already improved his grade point average from 40% to 85%. He has also mended friendships with students he bullied. He is consistent taking his behavior and academic folder home to his parents. He has also improved in reading comprehension. His grades in reading are As and Bs. With student support services, Rad has made changes in how he does his classwork and homework. Rad is a smart student who got off on the wrong track. With family problems mounting at home he was taken off focus. Rad was worried about his family and was concerned about his dad when he lost his job. After being homeless for 3 years Rad became a product of his environment. Social learning refers to the fact that we acquire much of our behavior by observing and imitating others within a social context. This is not a one-way flow of influence. According to social learning theory, people's behavior and environment influence each other. For example, at a societal level we are held accountable for obeying unpopular laws until we elect officials who will repeal or amend them, practice civil disobedience in order to influence legislators to change laws or rise up in revolt. Inherent in this complex social equation is the reciprocal influence of our behavior, our cognitive processes, and our social environment. Sometimes individual behavior prevails; at other times the environment prevails. Meanwhile, people perceive, judge, choose, and exercise a measure of self-control. (Kreitner & Luthans, 1984) Identifying a student at-risk early will give teachers the advantage of helping students before it's too late.

References

Brody, L. (2015, November 30). 'No Child Left Behind' Replacement Plan Shifts Power to States on Education. Retrieved October 26, 2016, from http://www.wsj.com/articles/no-child-left-behind-replacement-plan-shifts-power-to-states-on-education-1448928806

Driscoll, M. P. (2005). *Psychology of learning for instruction* (3rd ed.). Boston, MA: Pearson.

Kreitner, R., & Luthans, F. (1984). A social learning approach to behavioral management: Radical behaviorists "mellowing out". *Organizational Dynamics, 13*(2), 47-65. doi:10.1016/0090-2616(84)90018-4.

Ludwig, P. J., & Maehr, M. L. (1967). Changes in self-concepts in stated behavioral preferences. Child Development, 38, 453–469.

Meador, D. (2015, January 1). Title I. Retrieved October 25, 2016 from http://teaching.about.com/od/s-zteachingvocabulary/g/Title-I.htm

Woolley, S., & Woolley, A. (1999). Can We Change Teachers' Beliefs? A Survey about Constructivist and Behaviorist Approaches. Retrieved October 26, 2016, from http://www.eric.ed.gov/contentdelivery/servlet/ERICServlet?accno=ED430965

http://www.dallasisd.org/cms/lib/TX01001475/Centricity/domain/98/evaluation/11-12/finalrpts/EA11-301-2-SCE-Report-Final.pdf

Article 7

A Radical Approach To Managing Rad's Behavior

Abstract

Understanding how to provide differential instruction, identifying At-Risk students and creating behavioral plans are among key factors in the overall academic success of students. Teachers should provide instruction that model state objectives designed by the Education Agency for their state. When educators create curriculums they should align them with their state curriculum. The state curriculum details lesson objectives for each grade level, core subject and electives. Students will be tested for mastery of objectives for their grade level and core subject at the end of each school year. At-Risk students should be placed on an alternative plan to help them master state objectives. Students who consistently interrupt academic instruction are good candidates for behavioral plans. Teachers should provide differential instruction that match class demographics while making sure At-Risk students get extra help from student support services.

Rad's Behavioral Goals

In a previous conversation we learned Rad Nickels is a 4th grade student who needs to be identified as at risk. Rad is having problems with reading comprehension, social studies and science. He is also having problems in math from time to time, although it is his favorite subject. Rad and his family were also homeless for a period of 3 years when his father lost his job. The financial set back had a major affect on Rad's grades and attendance. Rad was angry about issues at home and took his frustrations out on other students in school. Rad bullied other students for various reasons. Rad's Language Arts teacher also felt that he may have some special needs. Initially, Rad's academic problems were left undetected. He was not given the help he needed in his core subject classes. His grades suffered and a progress report was not sent home to inform his parents before report cards came out. Teachers labeled him as a bad student. They did not investigate further why Rad was having problems in his classes. It is important to set behavioral and academic goals for him before it's too late.

The desired behavior for Rad is to improve his grades, decrease absences, improve reading comprehension, and follow the requirements in his behavioral contract. The first step is to identify at-risk students immediately by the criteria set by the school district. Next, Rad should be matched up with appropriate student support services available in the school, district and community. It is important to establish a solid teacher/parent relationship. Parents should also become allies with the teacher to help Rad improve behavior and academics. All parties committed to help Rad's behavior improve are obligated to sign a behavior conract. The behavior contract must include the teacher, student and parents' signature.

Vygotsky's Theory of Cognitive Development

Vygotsky's Theory of Cognitive Development works in concert with Rad Nickels' academic and behavioral issues.   Lev Vygotsky was a Russian psychologist who was born in 1896 and died in 1934. His work was largely unknown to the West until it was published in 1962. Vygotsky's theory is one of the foundations of constructivism. His theory includes three major points which are social interaction, the more knowledgeable other, and the zone of proximal development.

Vygotsky believed that social interaction played a key role in the process of cognitive development. Vygotsky felt social learning precedes development. He also states "Every function in the child's cultural development appears twice. First, on the social level, and later, on the individual level. It is seen first, between people (interpsychological) and then inside the child (intrapsychological)."

Next, the More Knowledgeable Other (MKO) refers to anyone who has a better understanding or a higher ability level than the learner, with respect to a particular task, process, or concept. The MKO is normally thought of as being a teacher, coach, or older adult, but the MKO could also be peers, a younger person, or even computers.

The last point in Vygotsky's theory is the Zone of Promixal Development (ZPD) which is the distance between a student's ability to perform a task under adult guidance and/or with peer collaboration and the student's ability solving the problem independently. According to Vygotsky, learning occurred in this zone.

Vygotsky's focus was on the connections between people and the sociocultural context in which they act and interact in shared experiences. According to Vygotsky, humans use tools that develop from a culture, such as speech and writing, to mediate their social environments. Initially children develop these tools to serve solely as social functions, ways to communicate needs. Vygotsky believed that the internalization of these tools led to higher thinking skills. (https://www.learning-theories.com/vygotskys-social-learning-theory.html)

The Impact of Vygotsky's Theory In The Classroom

Equipped with the knowledge of Vygotsky's Theory of Cognitive Development lesson activities will address Rad's academic and behavior problems. Rad's experience of being homeless for 3 years because his dad lost his job had a major impact on Rad's behavior and academics. Vygotsky's "Art As Theory Of

Emotion" provides clarity to emotional issues that Rad may have. According to Vygotsky, The imagination is the central expression of an emotional reaction. Aesthetics is a matter of delayed action. This can also be found in children's play. Children are able to control their actions and movements which are an aesthetic reaction which enhance the experience and intensity of the action. Children liberate their emotions through their imagination. Thus, they create their own interpretation of what they have experienced, in a way similar to when an author creates his work and a reader creates his interpretation of the work. (Lindqvist, 2003)

In order to get Rad help with his reading comprehension the reciprocal teaching instructional method will be used. It is used to improve students' ability to learn from text. With this method, teachers and students collaborate in learning and practicing four key skills such as summarizing, questioning, clarifying, and predicting. The teacher's role in the process is reduced over time.

Another instructional method that comes from Vygotsky's theory is called scaffolding and apprenticeship. With these two methods the teacher structures a task so that a novice can work on it successfully. These two methods will also be used to model lesson objectives for Rad's grade level and core subjects. Rad needs academic modeling of the lessons to help him get back on track reading above grade level. One effective strategy used in reading is called Tableau. The importance of visualizing ideas in texts has been well documented as a comprehension strategy. Tableau serves as an embodied form that takes the visualizing of images further and makes them concrete. This may have particular impact when dealing with more abstract texts, such as science information texts, and it says something about the uniqueness of drama as a agent of both abstract and concrete ideas. (Wagner, 1998) It will also help him with other subjects where he needs help.

Vygotsky's theories also feed into the current interest in collaborative learning, suggesting that group members should have different levels of ability so more advanced peers can help less advanced members operate within their ZPD. (https://www.learning-theories.com/vygotskys-social-learning-theory.html)

On The Right Path

As different teaching methods and strategies are used to help Rad get on track academically, he will also regain confidence. The instructional strategies previously mentioned will work in concert with daily lesson activities. Rad's reading comprehension will improve over time in all his core subjects. He will also be prepared to be tested at the end of the school year. Rad must show mastery of the state objectives in each core subject on his grade level. The behavioral contract in place must also be revisited on a daily basis with Rad. As Rad learns

how to work with his peers in hands on activities he will improve his behavior.

Hands on activities done in groups teach students how to work well with others.

With the support of educators, parents, student support services and peers, Rad will

succeed academically each year.

References

Branscombe, M. (2015, November). Showing, Not Telling. *Academic Journal, 69*(3), 321-329. Retrieved November 12, 2016, from http://eds.a.ebscohost.com/eds/pdfviewer/pdfviewer?sid=9d93b1c9-2146-4ce7-b6fc-685a9600e5a9@sessionmgr4009&vid=3&hid=4111

Lindqvist, G. (2003). Vygotsky's Theory of Creativity. *Creativity Research Journal, 15*(2-3), 245. Retrieved. November 12, 2016, from http://eds.a.ebscohost.com/eds/pdfviewer/pdfviewer?vid=2&sid=5797ddff-2eab-409c-ae58-0a6d8d5736e6@sessionmgr4010&hid=4111

Wagner, B. J. (1998). Educational drama and language arts: What research shows. Portsmouth, NH: Heinemann.

https://www.learning-theories.com/vygotskys-social-learning-theory.html

Article 8

Self Regulated Learning And Its Motivation

Abstract

All professionals should have the desire to master their craft. No matter what field is chosen it is imperative to be equipped with the most up to date knowledge, resources and tools. Mastering your craft takes time and involves much research to aid in learning. It continues to be my desire to learn everything about research methods. Research is for life long learners who enjoy learning new things to strenthen their performance. As an educator I look for efficient and successful ways to educate students who have different learning styles and abilities. Using Self-Regulated Learning strategies can simplify the process of research and understanding quantitative and qualitative research methods.

Research Process and Methods

No matter what field of study you have chosen, learning to do research is very important in any profession. Research can be a lengthy process but it yields great results. Learning about all aspects of your craft will equip you with the most up to date knowledge, resources and tools. It can also make you a valuable asset in your industry. One area where research is always needed is education. Studies and reports are always needed to get the most current data in the educational field.

According to Robert Trinchero (2014), in Education Sciences & Society, there is a required criteria that should guide the design of empirical research and the evaluation of research plans and reports. He says, the main idea is to demonstrate that educational research is instrinsically multi-method and mixed method. Qualitative and quantitative moments are present in all the research and the two approaches are closely interrelated. Qualitative and quantitative moments are present in all the research and the two approaches are closely interrelated. To overcome a paradigmatic view that impose the rigid separation between quantitative and qualitative approaches, five research principles are proposed such as the planning of the research, declaration of the theoretical "lenses" by which the researcher see and interprets the world, designing and documenting of the research plan, analysis of the data gathered and the definition of the logical extension of the research results.

Qualitative research is scientific research that seeks to answer a question and uses a predefined set of procedures to answer the question. Evidence is collected to produce findings that were not determined in advance. It also produces findings that are applicable beyond the immediate boundaries of the study. Qualitative research is effective in obtaining culturally specific information about the values, opinions, behaviors and social contexts of particular populations. Qualitative methods are also effective in identifying intangible factors such as social norms, socioeconomic status, gender roles, ethnicity, and religion. Data is gathered from participant observations, in-depth interviews and focus groups.

(www.ccs.neu.edu/course/is4800sp12/resources/qualmethods.pdf)

Quantitative research, however, is used to quantify the problem by way of generating numerical data or data that can be transformed into useable statistics. It is used to quantify attitudes, opinions, behaviors, and other defined variables – and generalize results from a larger sample population. Quantitative Research uses measurable data to formulate facts and uncover patterns in research. Quantitative data collection methods are much more structured than

Qualitative data collection methods. Quantitative data collection methods include various forms of surveys, online surveys, paper surveys, mobile surveys and kiosk surveys, face to face interviews, telephone interviews, longitudinal studies, website interceptors, online polls, and systematic observations. (Wyse, 2011)

Self-Regulated Learning

Self-Regulated Learning involves setting goals for learning. Students also monitor, regulate, and control their cognition. Their motivation and behavior is guided and constrained by set goals and the contextual features of the environment. (Pintrich, 2000, p. 453) Self-Regulated Learning also has a three phase cycle such as forethought, self reflection and performance.

During the forethought phase students set goals, choose learning and motivational strategies, they decide to participate and arrange environmental conditions. In the reflection phase students make judgements about learning performance, they infer causal attributions, evaluate goal attainment in ways that promote self-improvement. The last phase is performance where students employ strategies to focus attention, enhance encoding, and execute task, they track performance and judge progress toward goals. Students also adjust their performance as needed. (Driscoll, 2005)

Benefits of Self-Regulated Learning

When I apply Self-Regulated Learning while perfecting my skills on research methods I can see two benefits such as planning and self reflection. Taking on any topic to research involves a great deal of planning. It involves creating an outline that serves as a road map. This outline details what specific information will be covered in the research. Depending on which research approach used, qualitative or quantitative, each requires different data gathering instruments. Data gathering instruments include surveys, personal interviews, control groups, longitudinal studies, website interceptors, online polls, and observations. These tools are used to validate the information in the study.

Another benefit is self reflection. After completing a research project it always a good idea to do self reflection. During this time I objectively compare my final research to my initial outline. I check to see if I covered what I planned in the beginning in the research project. I also get feedback from others when they read my research. Sending out surveys and soliciting for comments about the research gives the author outside feedback that can be used improve the study.

According to Paris and Paris (2001), there are at least two metaphors guiding research and practice in the area of self-regulated learning, and each offers something of value to scholars and teachers alike. "One is the metaphor of acquisition, of learning new strategies and skills and applying them in school" (p. 96). In this view, teachers can teach strategies directly to learners, model good strategy use, and coach learners as to when and why strategies will be helpful to them. Modeling, in particular, is consistent with Bandura's views of self-efficacy and the observational learning processes that he proposed.

Challenges of Self-Regulated Learning

Although research is fun and exciting to life long learners who enjoy adding new information to their toolbox, it can also be boring, lengthy and tedious. The two challenges that can plague the joy of research is lack of patience for lengthy research projects and lack of technology literacy. When students cannot endure for the long haul they will give up on the task of research. It requires patience, organization, time, and planning. These requirements keep researchers from getting overwhelm with masses of information he or she may access over a period of time.

Taking time to plan and organize will keep some of the frustrations of research to a minimum. An outline can also keep researchers focused and on track.

Another challenge when using Self-Regulated Learning in research is lack of computer literacy. When a student lacks the technology skills and tools to do research on the computer it makes the research project more challenging. Research papers will not be typed and access to many online resources will be untouched. Lack of computer literaracy also frustrates the researcher. Spending valuable time trying to figure out how to access certain websites, learning how to operate the mouse or keyboard functions can be nerve wrecking. These challenges can be overcome by planning research projects ahead of time and taking a basic computer class to obtain necessary skills. Many colleges are now requiring students to pass a computer basics class before they register for classes.

Self-Regulated Learning In Research Methods

When I decide to research a topic I want to make sure it is something that interest me and will add to the research of other scholars. As I prepare for research I create an outline. The outline lists each topic of each paragraph that will be included in my paper. The topics in the outline are specific and narrow the information I will gather during research. During the planning phase I also write down places where I can get information such as the local library, personal interviews, newspaper archives, the internet, resources from state, national and international libraries. When I plan to get information from personal interviews I look up phone numbers and e-mail addresses. I call to set up a date and time for interviews and I also do a follow up e-mail. It is important to set up interviews via phone calls first. This method is more proactive than going to the physical location and finding out the person you want to interview is not available. It saves time, gas and disappointments.

When I tackle any research project I have specific goals in mind. I write down the specific topics I want to find out more information. Once I gather information I constantly refer back to my outline. I look to see if the information I gathered support the topics I chose. If the information from my research does not support my topics I do more research. I continue to look for newspaper and magazine articles that contain information that I need. I also search the internet to find information to support my topics. It is my goal to stick to the outline I initially drafted.

When gathering, arranging and putting the data all together in my research paper I make sure I have all the information that support my topic. I also find a quiet place to focus all my attention on my paper. When I get off track or topic I go back to edit out unnecessary information. I also proof read my own paper to make sure it covers my planned topic. When I have edited and completed the research paper I seek out peers to critique my work. Once I get feedback from others I correct errors and add any suggestions. When I am done I publish my research for others to read.

References

Driscoll, M. P. (2005). Psychology of learning for instruction (3rd ed.). Boston, MA: Pearson.

Paris, S. G., & Paris, A. H. (2001). Classroom applications of research on self-regulated learning. Educational Psychologist, 36(2), 89–101.

Pintrich, P. R. (2000). The role of goal orientation in self-regulated learning. In M. Boekaerts & P. R. Pintrich & M. Zeidner (Eds.), Handbook of self-regulation (pp. 452–502). New York: Academic Press.

Qualitative Research Methods: A Data Collector's Field Guide. (n.d.). Retrieved November 22, 2016, from www.ccs.neu.edu/course/is4800sp12/resources/qualmethods.pdf

Trinchero, R. (2014). Five research principles to overcome the dualism quantitative-qualitative. Education Sciences & Society, 5(1), 45-65. Retrieved November 22, 2016, from http://eds.a.ebscohost.com/eds/pdfviewer/pdfviewer?sid=0d5c474a-8442-456b-a152-d92eaec90266@sessionmgr4008&vid=0&hid=4210

Wyse, Susan. "Difference between Qualitative Research vs. Quantitative Research." Snap Surveys Blog. September 16, 2011. Accessed November 22, 2016. http://www.snapsurveys.com/blog/what-is-the-difference-between-qualitative- research-and-quantitative-research.

Article 9

Multicultural Curriculum Is Needed In All Classes

Abstract

The purpose of this project is to show that a multicultural curriculum is needed in all core and elective classes. Multiculturalism provides an opportunity for students to share their culture and experiences. It provides an avenue for students to work together to improve race relations. In "Intro to Media," students are taught two units called radio, speech and debate. Project based learning is utilized to allow students to participate in hands on learning. Students also incorporate their race, culture and experiences when they create their radio shows. The broadcasts are done in different languages and formats for different audiences. The objectives require students to produce written pieces for topics they choose for Radio, Speech and Debate. In the Radio unit, students write their own commercials to educate their audience on the benefits of their products. They also write commercials to persuade audiences to purchase their product. In the Speech and Debate unit, students write persuasive essays on controversial topics. Students are encouraged to use visual aids such as photos, banners, posters, graphs, sound bites, music, technology and audio scripts. Students incorporate their culture, background and experiences in their debate topics to reach various audiences. The project outlines instructional strategies developed, steps for implementation and the evaluation process to determine the success of the project.

Needs Analysis

In wake of the recent tragedy on July 7, 201 in Dallas, Texas where 12 police officers got shot and 5 eventually died, the unfortunate event is a result of a deeper problem of race relations.

This event was preceded earlier by two murders of African American men in Baton Rouge, Louisiana on July 5 and in Falcon Heights, Minnesota on July 6. The Black Lives Matter Organization was created earlier in 2012 after George Zimmerman was acquitted for the murder of 17-year-old Trayvon Martin. (Sidner & Simon, 2015) There are numerous documented police killings of African and Latino American men. (Adler, 2016) There has also been a rise in the killings of police officers in response to continued police brutality. The Blue Lives Matter Organization was also created in 2014 when two New York officers were killed as they sat in their police car. (Jauregui, 2014) This organization assists fallen police officers and their families. With this assessment it has been determined there is a critical need for race relations to improve in our nation. The change must come through an expanded multicultural curriculum that is implemented in our educational school systems across the United States.

Critical incident needs are failures that are rare but have significant consequences. They are also identified by analyzing potential problems. Identifying the root causes of poor race relations in the United States is essential when implementing Multicultural curriculums in education. (Morrison et. al, 2013) Multiculturalism in education will be the key to teaching students from Pre-k to 12th grade how to accept other races. Multiculturalism will also teach students to work with their peers who have different ethnic and cultural backgrounds. Teaching students early on how to respect and tolerate the differences of others will play its part in a bigger picture of race relations.

There is also an anticipated need for implementing Multicultural curriculums in classrooms nationwide. The need is anticipated to improve race relations and restore trust in humanity for years to come. Anticipated needs are a means of identifying changes that will occur in the future. Identifying such needs should be part of any planned change so that needed training can be designed prior to implementation of the change. (Morrison et. al, 2013)

In the past, our educational institutions were used to bring about change and equality in our society. Our future as a nation depends on our willingness to continue to reach into the racial cleavage that defines American society and change the racial contours of our world. In 1954, the federal government's brief in Brown v. Board of Education argued that school desegregation was a Cold War imperative, a necessary weapon to win America's battles overseas. Current events give us the same imperative to prove to enemy and ally alike that our commitment to justice is sincere. (Bond, 2015)

With the well-publicized police killings of unarmed Trayvon Martin and Michael Brown, the nation suffered a double loss twice when both cases ended with no convictions. Another case includes Eric Gardner who was also unarmed while being choked to death by a New York police officer. It is imperative that justice manifests for all races while purging out those who should be held accountable for their crimes. The late Dr. Martin Luther King Jr. is pleasantly remembered not just for his moral vision and advocacy for social justice but also for his spectacular oratorical elegance and philosophical profundity. One of his most erudite declarations is that "injustice anywhere is a threat to justice everywhere" (1963, p. 1). Dr. King goes on to say "I am cognizant of the interrelatedness of all communities and states... We are caught in an inescapable network of mutuality, tied in a single garment of destiny. Whatever affects one directly affects all indirectly." (p. 1) (Okafor, 2015)

Learner Characteristics

All demographics are included for learner characteristics in the identified need for

multicultural curriculums in schools across the U. S. These demographics include but are not

limited to race, culture, age, class, gender, grade level, etc. Teachers must meet the needs of all

learning styles in the classroom such as visual, auditory, and kinesthetic. Learning styles are

traits that refer to how individuals approach learning tasks and process information. Simply put,

some learners find certain methods of learning more appealing than others. For a long time, it has

been known that, rather than attending lectures and reading textual material, some individuals are

more comfortable learning from a visual approach to studying and others prefer to learn from

physical activities and the manipulation of objects. (Morrison et. al, 2013)

Activities should be designed for all three learning styles while incorporating the expanded

multicultural curriculum.   When Multiculturalism is not happening in classrooms it is because

teachers are not making it a priority and are not practicing diversity. Teachers are responsible

for including diverse content that will reflect the demographics of their classroom. It is

important that students see a reflection of themselves in the content taught by their teacher.

Diverse instructional content, presentations, workbooks, textbooks, and additional resources

should promote inclusion. Research and gathering diverse content and materials is an important

part of lesson planning. Teachers are responsible for what happens in their classroom. Whether

it is positive or negative it all rests on the teacher. The teacher is the leader, and students are

following the leader.

Objectives

Multicultural curriculums can be incorporated in all core subjects and electives. As teachers align their curriculums with state objectives, they will also include lesson activities to match the demographics of their classrooms. Every year I teach students detailed lesson content in Radio, Speech & Debate. Students also learn to incorporate their backgrounds and cultures while writing persuasive essays, commercials or speeches. In my "Intro to Media" class, I have written lesson objectives that reflect three domains such as cognitive, behavioral or psychomotor, and affective.

The cognitive domain includes objectives related to information or knowledge, naming, solving, predicting, and other intellectual aspects of learning. Bloom, Englehart, Furst, Hill, and Krathwohl (1956) developed a widely used taxonomy for the cognitive domain. The taxonomy is organized within two major groups such as simple recall of information and intellectual activities. Bloom labeled the lowest level as knowledge, and the higher mental abilities are classified into the five increasingly more intellectual levels of comprehension, application, analysis, synthesis, and evaluation. (Morrison et al, 2013)

In the Speech & Debate unit students will organize and present their ideas and information according to the purpose of the research and their audience. Students are expected to synthesize the research into a written or an oral presentation that compiles important information from multiple sources; develops a topic sentence, summarizes findings, and uses evidence to support conclusions; presents the findings in a consistent format; and uses quotations to support ideas and an appropriate form of documentation to acknowledge sources.

(http://ritter.tea.state.tx.us/rules/tac/chapter110/ch110b.html)

Next is the behavioral or psychomotor domain, it encompasses skills requiring the use and coordination of skeletal muscles, as in the physical activities of performing, manipulating, and constructing. Speech behavior in producing and projecting sound, coordinating sound and gestures. Giving instructions in a foreign language or presenting a literary reading with gestures for emphasis. (Morrison et al, 2013) Students will write 30 or 60 second persuasive texts to influence the attitudes or actions of a specific audience on specific issues. These short persuasive texts are called commercials. Students are expected to project their voice, use appropriate voice inflections, maintain eye contact with audience, use body language or non-verbal gestures to express their points in written pieces.

(http://ritter.tea.state.tx.us/rules/tac/chapter110/ch110b.html)

The last domain is called affective, which involves objectives concerning attitudes, appreciations, values, and emotions such as enjoying, conserving, and respecting. This area is typically believed to be very important in education and training. (Morrison et al, 2013) Students will work productively with others in teams. Students are expected to participate in student-led discussions by eliciting and considering suggestions from other group members and by identifying points of agreement and disagreement.

(http://ritter.tea.state.tx.us/rules/tac/chapter110/ch110b.html)

To help students master the writing objectives I use direct instruction and project-based learning activities. Direct instruction is used to present the lesson content for the Radio, Speech and Debate units. Direct instruction benefits all learners especially those who are auditory. Project based learning activities also benefits all students especially visual and kinesthetic learners. Students are required to produce written pieces for topics they choose for Radio, Speech and Debate. In the Radio unit, students write their own commercials to educate their audience on the benefits of their products. They also write commercials to persuade audiences to purchase their product. In the Speech and Debate unit, students write persuasive essays on controversial topics. Students are also encouraged to use visual aids such as photos, banners, posters, graphs, sound bites, music, technology and audio scripts.

Procedural Analysis Flowchart

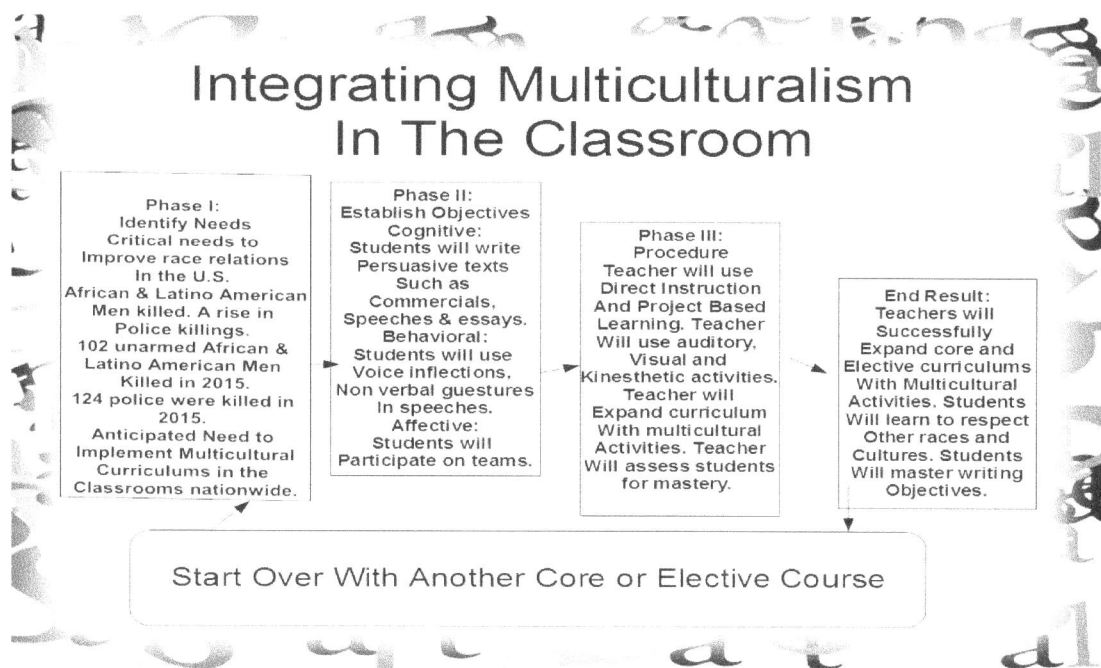

Integrating Multiculturalism In The Classroom

Phase I:
Identify Needs
Critical needs to
Improve race relations
In the U.S.
African & Latino American
Men killed. A rise in
Police killings.
102 unarmed African &
Latino American Men
Killed in 2015.
124 police were killed in
2015.
Anticipated Need to
Implement Multicultural
Curriculums in the
Classrooms nationwide.

Phase II:
Establish Objectives
Cognitive:
Students will write
Persuasive texts
Such as
Commercials,
Speeches & essays.
Behavioral:
Students will use
Voice inflections,
Non verbal guestures
In speeches.
Affective:
Students will
Participate on teams.

Phase III:
Procedure
Teacher will use
Direct Instruction
And Project Based
Learning. Teacher
Will use auditory,
Visual and
Kinesthetic activities.
Teacher will
Expand curriculum
With multicultural
Activities. Teacher
Will assess students
for mastery.

End Result:
Teachers will
Successfully
Expand core and
Elective curriculums
With Multicultural
Activities. Students
Will learn to respect
Other races and
Cultures. Students
Will master writing
Objectives.

Start Over With Another Core or Elective Course

Learner-Related Sequencing

In my course "Intro to Media," mediums such as Newspaper, Radio, Television, Speech & Debate, Books and Magazines are taught as units. For each unit a curriculum has been created and aligned with the Texas 6th grade writing objectives. Each unit also expands on the curriculum by incorporating lesson content that reflect the class demographics. In order for 6th grade students to grasp the material in each unit, the learning related sequencing scheme is used. Learning-related sequencing, suggests ways of sequencing the content based on learner characteristics identified in the learner analysis. This scheme considers the difficulty of the material, its appeal or interest to the learner, prerequisite information, and the learner's cognitive development. The learning related sequencing scheme includes five phenomenons which are identifiable prerequisites, familiarity, difficulty, interest, and development. (Morrison et. al, 2013)

The goal of this project is to require students to use writing mechanics to produce persuasive texts for radio scripts, speech and debate that represent and reach various cultures. Recent cases of police brutality and police relations with the community have prompted a critical need for race relations to improve in our nation. The change must come through an expanded multicultural curriculum that is implemented in our educational school systems across the United States.

Multicultural curriculums can be incorporated in all core subjects and electives. As teachers align their curriculums with state objectives they will also include lesson activities to match the demographics of their classrooms. School board members should also mirror the demographics of a school district. Change does not occur without a thoughtful and deliberate approach.

Having a holistic plan of action focused on board members' experience, competencies and demographics should encourage nominating committees to "go broad" and "dig deeper" to mine for new members and achieve diverse representation. (Trustee, 2016) Every year I teach students detailed lesson content in Radio, Speech & Debate. Students also learn to incorporate their backgrounds and cultures while writing persuasive essays, commercials or speeches. In my "Intro to Media" class, I have written lesson objectives that reflect three domains such as cognitive, behavioral or psychomotor, and affective.

The cognitive domain includes objectives related to information or knowledge, naming, solving, predicting, and other intellectual aspects of learning. Bloom, Englehart, Furst, Hill, and Krathwohl (1956) developed a widely used taxonomy for the cognitive domain. The taxonomy is organized within two major groups such as simple recall of information and intellectual activities. Bloom labeled the lowest level as knowledge, and the higher mental abilities are classified into the five increasingly more intellectual levels of comprehension, application, analysis, synthesis, and evaluation. (Morrison et al, 2013)

In the Speech & Debate unit students will organize and present their ideas and information according to the purpose of the research and their audience. Students are expected to synthesize the research into a written or an oral presentation that compiles important information from multiple sources; develops a topic sentence, summarizes findings, and uses evidence to support conclusions; presents the findings in a consistent format; and uses quotations to support ideas and an appropriate form of documentation to acknowledge sources.
(http://ritter.tea.state.tx.us/rules/tac/chapter110/ch110b.html)

Next is the behavioral or psychomotor domain, it encompasses skills requiring the use and coordination of skeletal muscles, as in the physical activities of performing, manipulating, and constructing. Speech behavior in producing and projecting sound, coordinating sound and gestures. Giving instructions in a foreign language or presenting a literary reading with gestures for emphasis. (Morrison et al, 2013) Students will write 30 or 60 second persuasive texts to influence the attitudes or actions of a specific audience on specific issues. These short persuasive texts are called commercials. Students are expected to project their voice, use appropriate voice inflections, maintain eye contact with the audience, use body language or non-verbal gestures to express their points in written pieces.

(http://ritter.tea.state.tx.us/rules/tac/chapter110/ch110b.html)

The last domain is called affective, which involves objectives concerning attitudes, appreciations, values, and emotions such as enjoying, conserving, and respecting. This area is typically believed to be very important in education and training. (Morrison et al, 2013) Students will work productively with others in teams. Students are expected to participate in student-led discussions by eliciting and considering suggestions from other group members and by identifying points of agreement and disagreement.

(http://ritter.tea.state.tx.us/rules/tac/chapter110/ch110b.html)

Based on the objectives mentioned, learner-related sequencing works best for "Intro to Media." Direct instruction will be used to teach the identifiable prerequisites for both units. Students will learn vocabulary words for the Radio Unit and the Speech and Debate Unit. They will learn the history of radio and the history of the criminal and civil justice systems. Students will also learn the importance of all cultures reflected in radio and the criminal and civil justice systems. They will learn the framework of a radio broadcast, a debate and a court trial.

Students will begin with the most familiar information and then progress to more advanced material. Students will begin with auditory and visual lesson activities that show examples in radio. Students will also be presented with examples of courtroom settings where speech and debate are utilized. Students will listen to D. L. Hugley and "The Steve Harvey Morning Show" radio broadcast, do an activity and discuss. They will also see a short clip of D. L. Hugley doing his radio broadcast, do an activity and discuss. Students will see a short clip of the radio broadcast "The Steve Harvey Morning Show," do an activity and discuss. They will see a sample video of a talk radio broadcast and discuss.

In the speech and debate unit, students will see a sample court trial in session, do an activity and discuss. They will see a short clip of the episode Law & Order, do an activity and discuss. Students will see a short clip of an episode "Judge Judy," do an activity and discuss. They will also see a sample video of a debate team performance, do an activity and discuss. These activities incorporate all learning styles and give students examples of radio, speech and debate.

As the course progresses, less difficult content is taught first then more advanced content is presented to students. Students will learn how to give appropriate feedback in speech and debate performances. Students will learn courtesy and etiquette rules of working on teams. They will learn how to choose appropriate topics to discuss. Students will also learn the types of written texts and essays. They will learn the rules of writing & mechanics. Students will learn how to research and gather sources for research topics. They will learn the speech & debate procedures. Students will also learn the steps of putting together a radio broadcast.

Students will also be given tasks that will create the most interest in radio, speech and debate. Students will perform a mock criminal trial. They will also perform a mock civil trial. Students will also learn how to put together and perform a radio broadcast. When students have successfully performed and created a radio broadcast and persuasive speech they will be assessed on their developed skills. The assessment will ensure that the learner has reached the appropriate developmental level before moving on to the next unit. Students will be graded on the performance of a radio show they create. They will also be graded on an argumentative speech they write. Students will be graded on their role and participation in a debate topic they are assigned.

Instructional Learning Strategies

Educators must find a way to teach the content so students can grasp the information. Using resources and materials that include audio, visual and kinesthetic activities will help students understand the lesson content. There are six categories of content. The categories are facts, concepts, principles, procedures, interpersonal skills, and attitudes. (Morrison et al., 2013) In the radio unit two generative categories are used such as recall and elaboration.

Recall is helpful for learning facts and lists for verbatim recall. Specific instructional strategies that facilitate recall include repetition, rehearsal (e.g., mental practice), review, and mnemonics. (Morrison et. al, 2013) When presenting lesson content students learn the steps to create a radio broadcast. The audio broadcast of the "D. L. Hugley," and "Steve Harvey Morning Show," allows students to listen to the order of a radio broadcast. Students must develop a mental picture of the steps or the order of each show. After students listen to the broadcasts they are asked to create a list of steps that will help them create their own radio show. The class will then discuss the steps they created. After the discussion a video presentation of the "D. L. Hugley," and "Steve Harvey Morning Show," will be shown to students to help them compare and contrast the steps they created.

Next students will get the chance to demonstrate what they learned. Elaboration requires learners to add their ideas or existing knowledge to the new information. Strategies that facilitate elaboration include generating mental images, creating physical diagrams, and relating existing knowledge to the new information. (Morrison, et. al, 2013) After the audio and visual class activities students will be shown the actual steps of creating a radio broadcast on the projector. Students will take notes and write each step down. The teacher will give students a chance to demonstrate they know the steps when they are given a quiz. The format of the quiz will list the steps with some of the steps missing for students to complete. Students will further demonstrate the steps when they create their own radio broadcast for their final class projects.

Examples of Instructional Strategies Based On Learner Analysis

There is a critical need for race relations to improve in our nation. The change must come through an expanded multicultural curriculum that is implemented in our educational school systems across the United States. Multicultural curriculums are used in "Intro to Media" to show a need for diverse communication to the masses. It is imperative that all cultures work together no matter what the issue may be.

Critical incident needs are failures that are rare but have significant consequences. They are also identified by analyzing potential problems. Identifying the root causes of poor race relations in the United States is essential when implementing Multicultural curriculums in education. (Morrison et. al, 2013) Multiculturalism in education will be the key to teaching students from Pre-k to 12th grade how to accept other races. Multiculturalism will also teach students to work with their peers who have different ethnic and cultural backgrounds. Teaching students early on how to respect and tolerate the differences of others will play its part in a bigger picture of race relations.

There is also an anticipated need for implementing Multicultural curriculums in classrooms nationwide. The need is anticipated to improve race relations and restore trust in humanity for years to come. Anticipated needs are a means of identifying changes that will occur in the future. Identifying such needs should be part of any planned change so that needed training can be designed prior to implementation of the change. (Morrison et. al, 2013)

The instructional strategies that can be used to help fulfill the critical and anticipated needs in this project are through lectures, powerpoint presentations, videos, short mp3 audio sound bites and outline given for students to follow during lecture.

Instructional Message

In my course "Into to Media, a pre-test is given to see what students already know about Media. A list of words are also given to see if students can identify what they mean. In order for students to understand words introduced and the lesson content in Media, pictures are used for unfamiliar vocabulary words. In this course there are many words in the lesson content sixth graders have never seen before. There are also some words that have unclear meanings such as disc jockey or d j. Other words include, news copy, news script, commercial, news feed, reporter, lead, hard news, opinion, facts, editorial, and interview. These words are clarified with students because they will see these words in the lecture content for radio, television, newspaper, speech and debate or books and magazines. Pictures will definitely help students match pictures with words they hear in the lecture. These pictures also help ESL or English Language Learners. While they learn English as a second language, they need pictures to reinforce learning English and media words they have never seen before.

Pictures are very important in the "Intro to Media" course. They provide illustrations of the lecture content discussed. Students can experience what is being taught in the lesson through pictures and illustrations. Pictures can provide concrete references for abstract terms presented in the text. Pictures can provide a decoration, representation, organization, interpretation, or transformation function in the text. When using pictures, it is important to guide the learners to use the images as they read the narrative. (Morrison et al, 2013)

Delivery Strategies for Learning Objectives

Using behavioral objectives for "Intro to Media" worked best while teaching elementary students. The function of the behavioral objectives informed students of what they needed to master. The objectives also served as guidelines and were displayed on the overhead during class. They were also listed on all lesson worksheets and activities.

Objectives perform two important functions for instructional designers, instructors, and teachers. First, they offer a means for the instructional designer to design appropriate instruction.

The objectives are also used to select and organize instructional activities and resources that facilitate effective learning. Second, objectives provide a framework for devising ways to evaluate student learning. Because written tests and performance activities are the major means of measuring student achievement, objectives should guide the design of relevant testing items and procedures. Thus, the writing and use of instructional objectives can have a worthwhile impact on improving both teaching and the resultant learning. (Morrison et al, 2013)

The content structure followed a definition and example format. Since "Intro to Media" was new to the students, a foundation was created with media definitions and examples. They were also used to connect other lesson content taught. Lectures and project-based learning were used to deliver the instruction. Other task attributes used in "Intro to Media" involved video lectures and guest speakers to teach students about the field of media.

Delivery Strategies for Instructional Context

Students get the full experience of "Intro to Media" when the classroom is transformed into a radio station or a debate setting. Students are also taken on field trips to radio and television stations. They can ask questions and get to see in real life what was taught in class lectures. Other environmental settings for "Intro to Media" include banners for Newspaper, Radio, Television, Books, Magazines, and Speech and Debate. Props are also brought into the classroom by the teacher and students when final performances or projects are presented. Transforming the classroom often when a new unit is covered keeps students interested and engaged. Students are eager to see what they will learn each semester.

Delivery Strategies for Instructional Strategies

When students learn the procedure for speech and debate, they also learn how to defend their position or argument. In speech and debate students learn how to use their critical thinking skills. They also learn how to solve problems that affect them and others. Diversity also is an acquired skill. Students must learn to work on projects with other races and cultures in grade school. If they don't learn how to work in harmony with others early on, it will be difficult when they enter the workforce. Firms have long relied on diversity training to reduce bias on the job, hiring tests and performance ratings to limit it in recruitment and promotions, and grievance systems to give employees a way to challenge managers. Those tools are designed to preempt lawsuits by policing managers' thoughts and actions. Yet laboratory studies show that this kind of force-feeding can activate bias rather than stamp it out. (Dobbin and Kalev, 2016) Students learn how to do research and use information they find in books, articles, blogs, newspapers, magazines, etc. to defend or refute a topic. Research skills will later help them in college and the workforce. Learning about diversity improves productivity. Diversity Organizations argues that ensuring a diverse workforce composition has tangible benefits for organizations. Rather than relying on touchy-feely arguments, Herring and Henderson present compelling evidence that directly links diversity to the bottom line. (2015) Students also learn how to project their voices when speaking in a presentation and on the radio. These skills will also help students when they interview for jobs, scholarships, or as a member of an organization. Overall, students learn skills in "Intro to Media" that will benefit them for the rest of their lives.

Evaluation Plan

The curriculum for "Intro to Media" is aligned with the Texas objectives for 3rd to 6th grade. The lesson content and activities are also aligned with specific objectives for ELAR. Once students are taught the lesson content they must be evaluated for objective mastery. Formative evaluation works best for "Intro to Media."

Formative evaluation is most valuable when conducted during development and tryouts. It should be performed early in the process, before valuable time and resources are wasted on things that aren't working. It is better to determine whether the instruction is effective early, while you have time to make modifications. If the instructional plan contains weaknesses, they can be identified and eliminated before full-scale implementation. Test results, reactions from learners, observations of learners at work, reviews by subject-matter experts, and suggestions from colleagues may indicate where there are deficiencies in the learning sequence, procedures, or materials. (Morrison et al, 2013)

"Intro to Media" is new to most students. When students are introduced to lesson content for Radio, Television, Newspaper, Books, Magazines, Speech and Debate teachers should observe for comprehension. Students need to understand the lesson material before advancing to other chapters or units. Formative evaluation gives teachers data to make modifications of lesson content, activities or tests when the initial curriculum is too difficult for students. Students must build foundational knowledge of the course before they are expected to grasp advanced content.

Both instructional designers and instructors need to use formative evaluation. For designers, the usual focus is the effectiveness of materials. Thus, if students perform poorly, the conclusion will be that the materials, not the students, are at fault (Hellebrandt & Russell, 1993). For instructors, the focus will be on the students. In "Intro to Media" the effectiveness of the materials and students are considered. When students grasp the content of the materials used and they are engaged it gives the teacher feedback for the success of the course.

The test instrument that works best in "Intro to Media" are objective tests. The test questions have one correct answer and thus can be objectively graded. I use multiple choice, matching, and true/false questions when testing for mastery of vocabulary, concepts and lecture content. I also use constructed response tests which include short essays or fill in the blank. These tests give students the opportunity to explain what they have learned from lesson content and activities. These tests are graded subjectively because students' answers will vary. Other testing instruments are used to test skills and behavior. The evaluation is on performance. Students are evaluated by the teacher and their peers on their radio shows and debate performances. Students' radio show performances are recorded and become apart of their portfolio.

The last testing instrument used is observation of instruction and assessment of behavior. Students are encouraged to use their culture, background and experiences in their projects and presentations. This requirement is used to educate students about other races and cultures. The teacher's goal is to implement a multicultural curriculum in the classroom and to improve race relations. Students are evaluated on their attitudes and behavior when learning about other races and cultures.

Test Questions

When students are taught the lesson content in "Intro to Media," they must be tested for mastery. Students are tested over the 6 levels of Bloom's Taxonomy which include knowledge, comprehension, application, analysis, synthesis, and evaluation. A five-question quiz will be given to students to check for understanding and mastery of lesson content.

Bloom's Taxonomy Level: Knowledge: Recall of specific information (Morrison et al., 2013)

1. List each step in the speech and debate process.

Bloom's Taxonomy Level: Comprehension: Lowest level of understanding (Morrison et al., 2013)

2. Explain the participants responsibilities in each step of the speech and debate process.

Bloom's Taxonomy Level: Application: Application of a rule or principle (Morrison et al., 2013)

3. Create a plan for your debate team of your responses for your affirmative and negative arguments.

Bloom's Taxonomy Level: Analysis: Breaking an idea into component parts and describing the relationships. (Morrison et al., 2013)

4. Compare and contrast the speech and debate process with the legal court room system.

Bloom's Taxonomy Level: Evaluation: Making Judgements (Morrison et al., 2013)

5. Defend your position on why you chose a specific debate topic to present.

Evaluation Approach

When teaching "Intro to Media" using objectives based formative evaluations is best. It allows modifications if necessary, when working with 3rd to 6th grade. It is important that students understand and master the writing objectives to prepare for state assessments. The writing objectives in "Intro to Media" are aligned with the curriculum written by the Texas Education Agency. Objectives-Based Studies involves investigating how well the instructional program is achieving its objectives. It uses summative and confirmative evaluations to determine the progress of students in completing instruction. Summative evaluates the effectiveness of a program immediately and confirmative evaluates a program over time. Objective Based formative evaluations are used as a basis for improving instruction when outcomes fall short of goals. They also use pre and post- tests that measure gains on measures of achievement and attitude. (Morrison et al., 2013)

Learning Theory

There are three learning theories applied in "Intro to Media." These theories include behaviorism, social and cognitive. A learning theory tends to be descriptive, explaining how learning takes place to achieve certain kinds of outcomes. Behaviorism is commonly associated with theorists such as B. F. Skinner, Ivan Pavlov, and E. L. Thorndike. It emphasizes maintaining desirable behaviors and eliminating undesirable behaviors by manipulating conditions in the environment. Such conditions essentially take the form of positive reinforcement or negative punishment consequences following a response. (Morrison et al., 2013)

The Behavioral Theory is applied when students are given stickers at the end of class if they participated in class discussions and activities. The stickers are also given if students displayed model behavior. The stickers were proof to their core classroom teachers that they did not get in trouble during elective classes. In the event that students did not get stickers at the end of class a note was sent to the core teacher to explain the undesirable behavior in the elective class. Next is the Social Learning Theory developed by Albert Bandura (1986). Social learning theory is best known for what its name implies—learning from others through observation and modeling. (Morrison et al., 2013) Social Learning is applied when students observe the teacher and their peers when presenting the process of speech and debate. Student also observe other students when they present their live radio broadcasts to the class. Students observe others so they will get ideas for their own presentations.

The last learning theory is called the Cognitive Learning Theory. Cognitive theorists are concerned with what occurs inside the mind—how we think, process information, remember and forget information, and acquire and use language to communicate. It also focuses on receiving, processing, and remembering information through reception and discovery learning approaches. (Morrison et al., 2013) This theory is applied when students take notes while the teacher is presenting lecture content in class. Students write down notes from the lecture to study and retain for assessments. Students also participate in class activities that reinforce the lecture content. Each year in "Intro to Media," students are taken on field trips to Radio and Television stations to observe and learn in a hands on environment. The field trips also reinforce what students have been taught in class from lecture content.

The two teaching strategies I use to apply all three learning theories are direct instruction and project based learning. Direct instruction is used for classroom lectures, activities, simulations, and discussions. Project based learning is used when students are assigned individual projects such as creating a radio broadcast. Students must use their writing skills to write out their radio show from beginning to end. They must write an introduction, what happens during the broadcast, and they must write a closing for their radio show.

Learning Theory Principles

There are three behavioral principles that can be applied to the project of implementing multiculturalism in "Intro to Media." The first behavioral principle states "Performance in less desirable activities can be increased by linking them with more desirable activities." This principle is important because many students do not like to read or write. Reading and writing is essential for education. To make reading and writing more interesting to students project based learning activities are implemented. Field trips and games are also used to engage students and keep their interest. There is a lot of reading and writing in "Intro to Media." Students must master English, Language Arts, and Reading Objectives. Writing conventions are also covered in the ELAR Texas Essentials Knowledge and Skills (TEKS).

The second behavioral principle that is used in "Intro to Media," states "Continuous reinforcement is superior to intermittent reinforcement for novice learners. Following acquisition learning intermittent reinforcement is superior in increasing resistance to extinction." "Intro to Media," is a new course with new and unfamiliar information to elementary students. Until students develop foundational knowledge positive reinforcement must take place. When students master writing objectives and lesson content they should receive immediate feedback. Students need to know at all times where they stand academically.

The last behavioral principle implemented states "Immediate reinforcers for approximate responses are effective for developing complex skills. It is always a good idea for teachers to connect with their students. When students have done a good job on their presentation, received a passing score on their test or went above and beyond with participation on their team, that student deserves praise from their teacher. When teachers cross paths with their students in the classroom and in the hallways they should give verbal praise or a pat on the back for their academic efforts. Teachers can also use immediate reinforcers when students are trying. If students almost have the correct answer when asked oral questions, teachers should probe further to help students arrive at the right answer.

Information Gaps

The information gaps in my project would include more detail about other job titles in radio besides announcers. There are people on staff that work behind the scenes in radio. The general manager, the interns, the weather announcer, the traffic announcer, the news announcer, the coordinator of programs that air at specific times, the reporters who go out and do the interviews and do research for the station. It is important to know about staff personnel that work behind the scenes because the on air talent can not run the station format alone. Learning about the other job titles in radio opens up more opportunities for students.

Another information gap in the project includes diversity training for administrators and teachers. Diversity training is necessary so teachers can learn why implementing a multicultural curriculum in the classroom is important. Diversity training will also include sensitivity training towards other races and cultures. Teachers should model what they teach in the classroom.

They should emphasize to students that working together with other races and cultures will be required on future jobs. Teachers should also reinforce that working together with other races and cultures creates peace and harmony.

Next Steps

To complete the delivery of instruction, the teacher will need media equipment such as video cameras, tape recorders, microphones, CDs, DVDs, books and materials for class lessons and projects. Other resources needed for the classroom include music cds, sample commercials, public service announcements, computers for students to type their scripts, soundbites, news feeds with news stories, banners, signs, table with two chairs for two anchors or announcers. Transportation and coordination of student lunches is needed for field trips. Field trips give students a real world experience in radio. Students get to see radio announcers do their daily job live on air. The radio stations we visit every year make accommodations for the teacher and students. Another field trip that needs to be scheduled is to an open courthouse. Students need to visit a civil proceeding that allows them to see the process used in court which is similar to speech and debate.

References

Adler, J. (2016, July 8). 7 lives that mattered: Reflections on a week's deadly toll. Retrieved July 8, 2016, from https://www.yahoo.com/news/seven-lives-that-mattered-reflections-on-a-weeks-deadly-toll-215803592.html

Bandura, A. (1986). Social foundations of thought and action: A social-cognitive theory. Englewood Cliffs, NJ: Prentice Hall.

Bond, J. (2015). With All Deliberate Speed: Brown v. Board of Education. *Indiana Law Journal, 90*(4), 1671-1681. Retrieved July 18, 2016. tt

Dobbin, F., & Kalev, A. (2016, July/August). Why Diversity Programs Fail. *Harvard Business Review, 94*(7), 52-60. Retrieved August 12, 2016.

Herring, C., & Henderson, L. (2015). *Diversity in organizations: A critical examination.* Routledge, NY: EPUB.

Jauregui, A. (2014, December 21). 2 NYPD Officers Dead In Brooklyn Shooting. Retrieved July 24, 2016, from http://www.huffingtonpost.com/2014/12/20/nypd-officers-dead-brooklyn-shooting_n_6360434.html

Morrison, G. R., Ross, S. M., Kalman, H. K., & Kemp, J. E. (2013). *Designing Effective Instruction* (7th ed.). Hoboken, NJ: John Wiley & Sons.

Okafor, V. (2015, March). Trayvon Martin, Michael Brown, Eric Garner, Et al.: A Survey of Emergent Grassroots Protests & Public Perceptions of Justice. *Journal of Pan African Studies, 7*(8), 43-63. Retrieved July 18, 2016.

Sidner, S., & Simon, M. (2015, December 28). The rise of Black Lives Matter: Trying to break the cycle of violence and silence. Retrieved July 24, 2016, from http://www.cnn.com/2015/12/28/us/black-lives-matter-evolution/index.html

Trustee, A. (2016, April). Diversifying Diversity. *Academic Journal, 69*, 8-9. Retrieved August 12, 2016. http://ritter.tea.state.tx.us/rules/tac/chapter110/ch110b.html

Article 10

Can College Students Of All Races, Cultures, Backgrounds, And Various Demographics Working Together On Projects In College Help Decrease Racism On A Bigger Scale?

Some people are still in denial when it comes to Racism in the United States. Racism is at its all time high in our society today. It is a degenerating disease that is seen as a public health hazard. Many can clearly see its affects, while others refuse to acknowledge that racism still exists. This country has a long history of mistreating humans based on race and skin color. For 400 years the United States engaged in the practice of slavery. Forced slave labor was used to build everything in this country from the ground up. This degrading practice of slavery was challenged on many occassions by the slaves and abolitionists. It wasn't until 1863, when President Abraham Lincoln signed the Emancipation Proclamation, that slaves were set free and slavery was abolished. Unfortunately, the affects of a slave system still has a major impact on how our country operates, moves and exists on a daily basis. This affect, rooted in old systems, must continue to be challenged to abolish laws that originated from the era of slavery. As a country we cannot move forward with the true essence of diversity if we are still operating under the control of a racist system.

Racism in the United States is outdated and should have died already. With the growing rate of migrants coming from other countries, America cannot continue to live in the shadows of its racist past, old beliefs and systems. The continued mistreatment of minority groups so Caucasian Americans can feel superior should be eradicated. U. S. laws should also be updated to reflect the multicultural society that currently exists. The face of America has changed to many colors. Various races and cultures has inundated U.S. soil. Our nation must embrace change to move forward successfully in the 21st century. Extensive research has been done to understand, evaluate and change racist beliefs and behaviors beginning with college students.

Purpose

In my study "Can College Students Of All Races, Cultures, Backgrounds, And Various Demographics Working Together On Projects In College Help Decrease Racism On A Bigger Scale?," I plan to show that the degenerating disease of racism still exists, beliefs determine behaviors, racism hinders progress and that racism can be decreased on a bigger scale by educating and providing opportunities for college students of all races, cultures, backgrounds and various demographics to work together on projects. Colleges and universities are fertile ground to promote and make changes in our society. It will be college students who graduate and take on positions in society that affect our world. These students need to be challenged on their belief systems when they enter college. They also need to be mentored and trained on diversity before they graduate or exit college. Diversity courses and activities promoting students of all races working together on projects is a preview of how students will interact in future jobs, careers and leadership positions that affect our society. Colleges and universities are microcosms of society and are therefore a logical place to address racial prejudice and prepare students to function in today's racially diverse society. As we move through the 21st century and educators embrace a more global and multicultural perspective, racial prejudice among students in higher education remains an issue worthy of further scientific investigation. (Chang, 2002)

Theories Used

My research will introduce several theories that exists within the studies used to develop my paper. These theories include the Social Learning Theory, Cognitive Apprenticeship, Situated Learning, Social Development, Psychological Behaviorism and Operant Conditioning Theory. (http://www.learning-theories.com) Social Learning Theory by Albert Bandura argues that people can learn new information and behaviors by watching other people. Also known as observational learning or modeling, this type of learning can be used to explain a wide variety of behaviors. Bandura also stated that learning would be exceedingly laborious, not to mention hazardous, if people had to rely solely on the effects of their own actions to inform them what to do. Fortunately, most human behavior is learned observationally through modeling: from observing others, one forms an idea of how new behaviors are performed, and on later occasions this coded information serves as a guide for action. (Cherry, 2014)

Social Learning Theory is a combination of Situated Learning and Social Development Theory. Situated Learning is a theory by Jean Lave. He argues that learning as it normally occurs is a function of the activity, context and culture in which it is situated. Social Development Theory by Lev Vygotsky, on the other hand, states social interaction plays a fundamental role in the development of cognition. This type of learning can also challenge students' beliefs while helping to develop their critical thinking skills to solve social problems.

The second learning theory is Cognitive Apprenticeship Theory which includes modeling, coaching, scaffolding, articulation, reflection and exploration. The third theory is called Psychological Behaviorism which states that a person's psychology can be explained by their observable behaviors. Psychology includes personality, learning and emotions. The last theory that exists within my research is the Operant Conditioning Theory which is the process used to modify behavior through positive and negative reinforcement. These theories working in concert together will help develop and support my research question, "Can College Students Of All Races, Cultures, Backgrounds, And Various Demographics Working Together On Projects In College Help Decrease Racism On A Bigger Scale?"

Summary of Literature Used

The study called "The Inclusive University: Helping Minority Students Choose a College and Identify Institutions that Value Diversity," by Carol Elam and Gilbert Brown uses the Cognitive Apprenticeship Theory. This study seeks to educate and give advice to minority high school students transitioning to college. The study focuses on helping minority students choose a college that is inclusive and values diversity. These variables matter in the overall success of minority students. An inclusive university provides an environment that accommodates, opportunities, equal access, support services on campus, and equality in interaction with faculty and peers. Students are not judged by racial, ethnic, social, or economic backgrounds. Although excellent advice was given on how to choose a college, the authors failed to mention policies on how issues are handled by college administration when hate crimes occur. Administration should educate students about hate crimes and also provide a hotline number to report incidences.

The authors provide 6 principles to teach students how to choose a college. Students should check college communication on diverse expectations. The expectations for students must be clear. They should also check to see if staff, faculty and administrators practice diversity. Students should also look for diversity in curriculums and if diversity training is provided for staff, faculty, and students. The last thing students should look for is a policy on inclusion for social and professional organizations. College campuses should also work on recruiting students of color. University leadership must create and implement a plan that is comprehensive and has energetic efforts to identify students from all backgrounds. (CPRJ, 1993) Networks in the community can identify young students of academic excellence who may also be first generation college students. These networks include guidance counselors, minority church leaders, Greek organizations, and action councils in the community. The network can also include alumni students who had positive experiences during their undergraduate studies.

A second study called "Interracial Friendships in College," by Carmargo, Stinebrickner & Stinebrickner uses the Situated Learning Theory. The authors provide evidence about interracial friendships at different stages of college and also new evidence about the observed patterns of interaction. They discovered black and white students are very compatible as friends and when roommates are chosen randomly with different races, they are as likely to become friends than those who are roommates of the same race. This study used longitudinal data which was taken from the Berea Panel Study conducted at Berea College. Surveys and observations were done to get information on students' experiences with their assigned roommates. The study also concluded that policies such as affirmative action caused students of different races to interact.

The research failed in the area of allowing students to pick their own roommates. Data could be collected about giving students a preference. This could also provide an opportunity for researchers to analyze data to see if students would chose a roommate of a different race.

Researchers could also interview those students who chose a roommate of a different race to find out the reason for their choice.

A third study called "Why Are All the White Students Sitting Together in College? Impact of Brown v. Board of Education on Cross-Racial Interactions among Blacks and Whites," by Strayhorn and Johnson uses the Psychological Behaviorism Theory. This study analyzes data from surveys taken from a national sample of 1,227 Black and White college students to examine frequent interactions with other races. The study also examined the data's influence on how welcomed students felt at their college campuses. The authors used the Supreme Court case of 1954, Brown v. Topeka Board of Education to bring their research findings into perspective. In the study the authors also point out the benefits of diversity. There are also three ways that institutions cause diversity to happen such as structural diversity, classroom diversity, and interactional diversity. The study finds that cross racial interactions in college vary across racial groups with Blacks reporting more frequent cross racial interactions than Whites. Although this study only analyzed the interactions between White and Black racial groups, it did not examine other races such as Latinos, Asians, Native Americans and other demographic groups. (Strayhorn & Johnson, 2014)

A fourth study called "Is Integration a Dream Deferred? Students of Color in Majority White Suburban Schools," by Thandeka Chapman uses both Psychological Behaviorism and Operant Conditioning Theory. In this study almost 100 students of color in four suburban districts are interviewed. The author of this research seeks to find out what type of relationship students have with school adults. The author also examines how the relationship has an impact on students' educational experiences, college and career selections. Students were interviewed to report their experiences with teachers. Black students in predominately white schools said they were

mistreated and talked down to. Students also felt disrespected because of their skin color. The

relationship that teachers have with their students also impact how students connect with school,

their course accessibility in high school, and future college options based on courses listed on

their transcripts. In this study students also reported the negative comments that came from

teachers and their lack of support toward students of color. The study also found that teachers

and counselors set low expectations for black students. They did not encourage black students to

seek higher educational goals. Although integration of schools took place with the passage of

the 1954 Brown v. Topeka Board of Education, racism in education still exists.

More research is needed in predominately White schools to fully understand the nature and

extent of racism at these schools. The research that is available on this topic comes from the

perspective of students. Qualitative methods has put a spotlight on the issues at majority White

schools. On the other hand, quantitative data must be collected to fully show the depth and

breadth of this issue. While school demographics are publicly available, racial breakdowns for

the tracks, and how many students attend college from the lower tracks, in each school are

unavailable. A statistical analysis of school tracking and students career paths by race and track

would demonstrate the outcomes of tracking in these school settings.

In a fifth study titled "U.S. College Student Activism during an Era of Neoliberalism: A

Qualitative Study of Students Against Sweatshops," it uses the Cognitive Apprenticeship

Theory. College students at Beautiful River University worked together to bring awareness of

the poor treatment of labor workers. Students made activism a top priority, they recruited new

members and gained friendships, and they also became an international network. Student activism is influenced by the neoliberal environment at Beautiful River University and at the same time student activists are working to resist and counter such practices. (Dominguez, 2009)

Student activism is work done by students to impact political, economic, environmental and social change. Student activism often focus on educational improvement, or specifically on pressuring educational institutions to change curricula, funding schemes, and to amplify student voices and representation in decision making (Rhoads 2000; Altbach 1968, 1970). The participants in this research project are members of a branch of United Students Against Sweatshops (USAS). USAS is an international movement of campuses and individual students fighting for sweatshop-free labour conditions and workers' rights. USAS defines the notion of a "sweatshop" broadly, arguing that sweatshops are not limited to the apparel industry, but include a plethora of low-paid labour positions, such as outsourced custodial workers on university campuses.

In this study it shows students working together to counter-act businesses who do not practice fair labor working conditions. These businesses compete in the marketplace with their bottom line of making money. Supporters of neoliberalism argue that free markets, free trade, and the unrestricted flow of capital will produce the greatest social, political and economic good. (Hartwich, 2009) Students Against Sweatshops actively stand up for these workers who are treated unfairly on their jobs. Students of all races and diverse backgrounds can learn to work together for a common cause that affects everyone. When students work together for a greater cause than themselves it can decrease racism on a larger scale. Although this study showed college student activism, it was limited to the findings exclusively on one college campus,

Beautiful River University. The study should have also included an equal number of members from each race participating in activism on the university campus.

The last study I looked at is called "Racial Prejudice In College Students: A Cross-Sectional Examination," by Gassner and McGuigan. This study uses the Social Learning Theory. In this study it included research findings by authors on seniors and freshmen who completed or began their diversity requirement courses for their majors. The research gathered statistical numbers from student surveys to report the reduction in blatant racism when students completed a diversity course. There were high levels of racism from students who had not completed a diversity course. Gassner and McGuigan's research supports that requiring students to take diversity courses as a part of their major helps decrease racism on a larger scale.

A five-point Likert scale adapted from the Modern Racism Scale created by McConahay, Hardee, & Batts in 1981 measured the student's level of racial prejudice. Statements included: Blacks have more influence upon school desegregation plans than they ought to have, and Blacks are getting too demanding in their push for equal rights. Additionally, a two item survey adapted from the College Students Experience Questionaire asked students to report how often they became acquainted with students from a different race (1=Never, 4=Very often) and how serious their discussions were with the students from different racial backgrounds. Results showed that students beginning their diversity requirements judged African Americans more harshly and displayed higher levels of prejudices (m=3.749) than students who had completed their diversity requirements (m=3.487). In addition, the students who had stronger negative feelings toward African American were less likely to have serious discussions with individuals from any different racial background. The study was limited by focusing exclusively on racial prejudice towards African Americans and no other minority group. (Gassner and McGuigan, 2014)

Each study presented is background knowledge and evidence that supports my research topic. Racism is subtle. It is a silent killer of diversity and progress in employment, housing, education, civil rights, etc. You cannot see a person's heart, belief or motive unless it identifies itself with an action. It is important to present studies that point out the affects of racism, what racism is and that it needs to be eliminated. Other research also provides solutions of various races working together in harmony. Colleges and universities serve as laboratories of change. When races come together for a common cause or charity the color of one's skin should become a non issue. With everyone working together, racism will soon be eradicated and a memory of the past.

References

Altbach, P. (1968). Turmoil and transition: Higher education and student politics in India, New York: Basic Books.

Altbach, P. (1970). Student movements in historical perspective: The Asian case. Youth and Society, 1, 333-57.

Camargo, B., Stinebrickner, R., & Stinebrickner, T. (2010). Interracial Friendships in College. *Journal of Labor Economics, 28*(4), 861-892. Retrieved April 21, 2016

Chang, M. J. (2002). The impact of an undergraduate diversity course requirement on student's racial views and attitudes. The Journal of General Education, 51(1), 21-42.

Chapman, T. (2014). Is Integration a Dream Deferred? Students of Color in Majority White Suburban Schools. *The Journal of Negro Education, 83*(3), 311-326. Retrieved April 21, 2016.

Cherry, K. (2014, November 24). Social Learning Theory: How People Learn Through Observation. Retrieved April 20, 2016, from http://psychology.about.com/od/developmentalpsychology /a/sociallearning.htm

Committee on Policy for Racial Justice. (1993). The Inclusive University. Washington, D.C.: Joint Center for Political and Economics Studies.

Dominguez, R. F. (2009). U.S. College student activism during an era of neoliberalism: A qualitative study of students against sweatshops. The Australian Educational Researcher Aust. Educ. Res., 36(3), 125-138. Retrieved April 11, 2016.

Elam, C., & Brown, G. (2005). The Inclusive University: Helping Minority Students Choose a College and Identify Insititutions that Value Diversity. *Journal of College Admission,* (187), 14-17. Retrieved April 21, 2016.

Gassner, B., & McGuigan, W. (2014). Racial Prejudice In College Students: A Cross-Sectional Examination. *College Student Journal, 48*(2), 249-256. Retrieved April 11, 2016.

Hartwich, O. (2009). Neoliberalism: The Genesis of a Political Swearword. Retrieved April 14, 2016 from http://www.cis.org.au/temp/op114_neoliberalism.pdf

Rhoads, R. (2000). Freedom's web: Student Activism In An Age Of Cultural Diversity. Baltimore: The Johns Hopkins University Press.

Strayhorn, T. L., & Johnson, R. M. (2014). Why Are All the White Students Sitting Together in College? Impact of Brown v. Board of Education on Cross-Racial Interactions among Blacks and Whites. *The Journal of Negro Education, 83*(3), 385-399. Retrieved April 21, 2016.

Vygotsky, L.S. (1978). Mind in Society. Cambridge, MA: Harvard University Press.

Can College Students Of All Races, Cultures, Backgrounds, And Various Demographics
Working Together On Projects In College Help Decrease Racism On A Bigger Scale?

http://www.learning-theories.com

http://www.learning-theories.com/operant-conditioning-skinner.html

http://www.learning-theories.com/psychological-behaviorism-staats.html

http://www.learning-theories.com/cognitive-apprenticeship-collins-et-al.html

http://www.learning-theories.com/situated-learning-theory-lave.htm

http://www.instructionaldesign.org/theories/situated-learning.html

http://www.instructionaldesign.org/theories/social-development.html

Can College Students Of All Races, Cultures, Backgrounds, And Various Demographics
Working Together On Projects In College Help Decrease Racism On A Bigger Scale?

Article 11

Accountability Should Be The Measuring Stick In Education

It is amazing how hypocritical our U.S. educational system has become while praising and promoting education, yet failing to hold the system and its key players accountable for equipping students for the 21st Century. Accountability should be the measuring stick in Education. The U.S. Department of Education, state agencies, school districts, administrators, teachers, students and parents alike should all have a part when it comes to accountability. When accountability breaks down at any level everyone suffers because of the weak link. It is imperative that the importance of education is upheld at all levels so the standard of excellence will not be lost.

Educators and students remain under the spotlight when it comes to state mandated assessments. Teachers and students are under pressure to produce desired outcomes for school districts and states. When things don't go as planned all key players are pointing fingers to place blame on someone else. Until everyone involved in the U.S. Educational System take responsibility and improve their deficiencies, placing blame somewhere else will continue to be the norm.

Testing requirements in the No Child Left Behind Law has been under fire for some time now. Educators, administrators, parents, and students alike are not pleased with the state mandated assessments and procedures. Students are still being left behind despite well planned out curriculums of each state. Severe consequences result in teacher job loss and students repeating the same grade. Educators, administrators, students and parents are looking for

alternatives that yield results and ease the NCLB testing requirements.

3 Key Reasons For Assessment Accountability

There are three reasons to re-evaluate the No Child Left Behind testing process before it is

done away with. The testing for No Child Left Behind is not all negative. There are a lot of

positive factors that come with the No Child Left Behind Law. For example, NCLB did a good

job of making data an important part of the school improvement process and of exposing the

persistent achievement gaps at even the most high achieving schools. (Starr & Spellings, 2014)

The No Child Left Behind Law introduced accountability for states, school districts, teachers

and students. Teachers need to be held accountable for covering all the state objectives with

students to prepare them for their state exams at the end of the year.

We also need to take a closer look at deficiencies at all levels in education. We should look at

student achievement, teachers, administrators, and state accountability when it comes to the No

Child Left Behind testing process. Once these things are evaluated, we need to work on

improving where we are failing in each area.

Assessment research for the No Child Left Behind Law and Every State's Curriculum for their

school districts need to be evaluated to uncover deficiencies. This suggestion is recommended

because states, school districts, administrator and teachers can no longer continue to blame low

test scores, school sanctions, cheating and no meeting requirements detailed in state curriculums

on the No Child Left Behind Law. A prime example would be the U.S. Education Department graning waivers from the No Child Left Behind Law to states who requested them. This gave states an opportunity to create their own curriculum and accountability measures that were comparable or exceed the No Child Left Behind Requirements. The State of Washington was the first to lose its waiver because it failed to meet the requirements in the waiver. The state of Washington was given ample time to meet the requirements. They now have to go back under the No Child Left Behind Curriculum and meet requirements that they should have met from the beginning.

The U.S. Department of Education provided waivers to release states from the requirements of the NCLB law. The waivers have been successful in some states and other states are failing to meet the alternative requirements. For example, Texas and Washington were among the 43 states that were approved for waivers. These states were released from the strict requirements of the No Child Left Behind Law. In exchange they would be responsible for carrying out certain actions in support of key education reforms.

States are required to put in place teacher and principal evaluation and support systems that take into account information on student learning growth based on high-quality college and career-ready (CCR) State assessments as a significant factor in determining teacher and principal performance levels, along with other measures of professional practice such as classroom observations. These systems also require that all teachers and principals receive robust, timely, and meaningful feedback on their performance and support in order to inform and improve instruction so that all students meet the expectations of new CCR standards. Including student learning growth as a significant factor among the multiple measures used to determine performance levels is important as an objective measure to differentiate among teachers and principals who have made significantly different contributions to student learning growth and closing achievement gaps. (http://www2.ed.gov/policy/eseaflex/secretary-letters/wad6.html)

Texas has maintained its commitment to keep its Flexibility Waiver. The Texas Education Agency has successfully drafted a solid curriculum that has stood the test of time. Before the installation of Texas Governor Greg Abbott on January 20, 2015, the previous Governor Rick Perry rejected the Common Core State Standards in 2014. Texas was one of onlyfive states that did not choose to adopt the Common Core State Standards. Instead,Texas chose to retain itsTexas Essential Knowledge and Skills (TEKS) standards. TEKS meet or exceed CCSS in the areas of mathematics and English and Language Arts. To further demonstrate their independence from CCSS, HB462 made use of Common Core related materials or developing assessments based on Common Core illegal beginning in 2014.(Burkett, 2014)

Washington, on the other hand, received a letter from the Secretary of the U.S. Department of Education revoking its Flexibility Waiver. Secretary Arne Duncan, penned a letter to Washington's Superintendent of Public Instruction, Randy Dorn notifying him that Washington's flexibility will end with the 2013–2014 school year. Washington was unable to take the steps necessary to fulfill the requirements of the waiver commitment even after the state was given an additional school year (2012–2013) to do so, it was placed on high-risk status on August 14, 2013. Washington's high-risk designation specified that the State must submit, by May 1, 2014, final guidelines for teacher and principal evaluation and support systems that meet the requirements of ESEA flexibility, including requiring local educational agencies (LEAs) to use student achievement on CCR State assessments to measure student learning growth in those systems for teachers of tested grades and subjects. Washington's request for an extension in the

March 27, 2014 letter to Secretary Arne Duncan indicates that the State was unable to provide

such guidelines. Washington and its Local Education Agencies (LEAs) must resume

implementing the requirements of Title I of the ESEA, as amended by the No Child Left Behind

Act of 2001 (NCLB), as well as all other ESEA requirements that were waived under ESEA

flexibility, for the 2014–2015 school year. (http://www2.ed.gov/policy/eseaflex/secretary-

letters/wad6.html)

Teachers are also failing in their efforts to educate students and prepare them for college.

Educators are under tremendous pressure to ensure that their students perform well on tests.

Unfortunately, this pressure has caused some educators to cheat. The purpose of this study was

to investigate the types of, and degrees to which, a sample of teachers in Arizona were aware of,

or had themselves engaged in test-related cheating practices as a function of the high-stakes

testing policies of No Child Left Behind. A near census sample of teachers was surveyed, with

valid responses obtained from about 5 percent, totaling just over 3,000 teachers. In addition, one

small convenience sample of teachers was interviewed, and another participated in a focus

group. Data revealed that cheating occurs and that educators can be quite clever when doing so.

(Amrein-Beardsley, et al, 2010)

Relevance of your assessment topic for K-12 assessment goals

The previous background information provides relevance for the topic of accountability in

education and the assessment process. Shining a light on teacher accountability when it comes to

covering the required state objectives throughout the school year to prepare students for their

state mandated tests. There should be documentation that proves that teachers covered required

objectives with students. When teachers fail to do what they are required to teach, it is unfair to expect students to succeed at state required tests. The Texas Education Agency has drafted a state curriculum for all school districts in Texas to follow. Texas has an educational plan for every core subject that is tested with the state mandated test called the State of Texas Assessments of Academic Readiness (STAAR). The plan has been drafted and educators need to become more efficient and strategic at working the plan. Texas has the Texas State Literacy Plan, Dallas ISD school district has identified its At-Risk Students so educators can draft curriculums to meet the needs of those students, Texas has also drafted its plan to detail what should be included in a state mandated curriculum to make sure students are college ready.

Teacher accountability for student assessments should be monitored throughout the year. Waiting for test results at the end of the year is too late to turn things around for teachers and students. In order for success to come from any educational policy or law accountability must be demanded in the assessement process throughout the year. Teachers should be required to show documented evidence that objectives were covered and students were tested for mastery. The graded test papers are documented evidence to show student progress. It helps teachers and students by giving a preview of how students will do at the end of the year on state mandated tests. Assessments over state objectives throughout the year keeps teachers and students accountable.

Accountability systems include education laws handed down to the states from the U.S. Department of Education, outlines of states' mandated curriculums handed down to school districts from state education agencies, states mandated assessments and procedures, and the rewards and consequences of achievements and failures.

Before states request waivers from the No Child Left Behind Law they should look at the benefits and overall purpose of the law. Many have voiced their objection to the NCLB law because funding is tied to student test results in each state. Students must show adequate performance based on state objectives they mastered during the year.

Dallas ISD uses the state mandated TEKS curriculum and the State of Texas Assessments of Academic Readiness (STAAR). The school district also utilizes the Texas State Literacy Plan to accomplish academic success in reading for K to 12th grade. The literacy plan include valid and reliable assessments, including the use of assessments that are appropriate for English language learners which are used to gather information. Data analysis informs all levels of decision making, systematic, explicit, and coherent instruction utilizing evidence-based instructional materials and practices in reading and writing is provided following the Texas Essential Knowledge and Skills in English and Spanish, the English Language Proficiency Standards across all grade levels and content areas, and the College and Career Readiness Standards for every school-age student. Effective instruction, differentiated based on assessed needs, is provided to all learners through a response to intervention framework. Classroom teachers, interventionists, and specialists in dyslexia, gifted and talented education, special education, and bilingual and English as a second language programs coordinate to meet the diverse needs of all learners, achievement goals are clearly defined, and progress is monitored at every age/grade level. (https://tslpresource.org/lasers/texas-state-literacy-plan-overview)

Dallas ISD has detailed and provided their criteria for At-Risk students in their State Compensatory Education Program. At-Risk students are grades PK-3 who did not perform satisfactorily on a readiness test during the current school year, grades 7-12 who did not maintain an average equivalent to at least 70 on a scale of 100 in two or more subjects during the semester, a student who was not advanced from one grade level to the next, students who did not perform satisfactorily on an assessment instrument administered under TEC Chapter 30, Sub-chapter B, and has not in the previous or current school year, and a student who is pregnant or is a parent. Students are also at-risk if they have been placed in an alternative education program during the preceding or current school year, have been expelled during the preceding or current school year; are currently on parole, probation, deferred prosecution, or other conditional release, and was previously reported through PEIMS to have dropped out of school. Other at-risk students include students of limited English proficiency (LEP), those who are in custody or care of the Department of Protective and Regulatory Services. Students who are homeless, those who reside in a residential placement facility, detention facility, a substance abuse treatment facility, emergency shelter, psychiatric hospital, halfway house, or foster group home. (http://www.dallasisd.org/cms/lib/TX01001475/Centricity/domain/98/evaluation/11-12/finalrpts/EA11-301-2-SCE-Report-Final.pdf)

Integrating Technology In The Classroom

Although each state is responsible for drafting a strong accountability systems, they should also use software programs that require teachers to input testing data and daily grades for their students. The software will keep track of student progress. Accountability systems also include school district websites that have parent portals. Parents can check their child's grades, test scores, behaviors and accomplishments. States have been successful at drafting broad accountability systems for their school districts. One area of improvement is to hold teachers and students accountable throughout the year. Software programs that monitor teacher and student activity is a good place to start.

Dallas ISD can also improve student assessment scores by implementing technology in their curriculums. With more schools statewide not meeting Annual Yearly Progress, many educators and administrators feel that students are not engaged in the curriculum and have not been motivated to learn the material they learn in the classroom. By using modern technologies that students are familiar with, teachers can integrate similar technologies and use these to their advantage as an attempt to motivate and engage learners. Starting at a young age, children are introduced to visual learning. Even babies today are subjected to technological toys such as baby mp3 players, video equipment, and computer programs developed to give them a head start on their learning. (Rafool, et al, 2012)

Digital technologies permit users unprecedented control over the content they consume and the place in and pace at which they consume it. At the heart of effective technology integration practices, digital technologies offer learners greater opportunities to be more actively involved in the learning experience. (Vega, 2013)

Effective teachers model and apply the ISTE Standards for students as they design implement, and assess learning experiences to engage students and improve learning; enrich professional practice; and provide positive models for students, colleagues, and the community. All teachers should meet the following standards and performance indicators. (http://www.iste.org/standards/iste-standards/standards-for-teachers)

Educators can use software that specifically tracks the mastery of each reading objective that is outlined in the Texas Essentials Knowledge and Skills for each grade level. The suggested technology software program is a Universal Online Reading Program with an Accountability System Tracker working in concert with the Texas State Literacy Plan.

Educators can also utilize release tests taken by students in the previous school years to help prepare students in the current year. Teachers can allow students to take timed tests on the computer at school over reading objectives taught that week. Each student can work independently on their assessments and once they have mastered an objective they can advance to the next. Computerized tests are benefitual for both students and teachers because students don't have to wait for their results and teachers can give immediate feedback.

Educators can also utilize technology by creating an intranet website for students. The intranet website will be for an educator's core subject and for each class the educator teaches. The intranet website will allow students to create their own use names and password for the site. The educators can put links to different websites that can help students at home and at school. Students can review and practice lessons taught in the class, play educational games, and research additional information on current and future class objectives.

It is no doubt that some educators are gifted to be teachers and some are not. Teaching is a calling, it is a passion, a duty, an obligation, it is a mission. When teachers embrace their passion they go above and beyond to help students excel academically. All students have the potential to do great. It takes the right teacher who knows how to reach students where they are and bring them up to their highest potential. Depending on high stakes testing alone will not help student's academic progress. High stakes testing is not useful as an assessment to improve learning. Because the tests are administered and scored at the end of the school year, they are of little assistance to teachers who want to identify students in need of help. The results are reported as single scores that provide no diagnostic information to help a teacher work with a student. (Levine & Levine, 2013)

When all key players in U.S. Education take responsibility for their role in educating students there will be change and progress. Congress is responsible for passing education laws that promote academic excellence and are practical for all involved. State Education Agencies are responsible for drafting state curriculums that align with the current education law. School districts are then responsible for implementing the curriculum. Teachers must also create lesson plans that align with state mandated curriculums and students must show mastery of the objectives in each tested core subject for their grade level. When everyone is held accountable for their part in education, pointing fingers and placing blame else where will be a thing of the past.

References

Amrein-Beardsley, A., Berliner, D., & Rideau, S. (2010, June 14). Cheating in the First, Second, and Third Degree: Educators' Responses to High-Stakes Testing. Retrieved November 16, 2015, from http://www.eric.ed.gov/contentdelivery/servlet/ERICServlet?accno=EJ895618

R. Burkett, J. (2014, March 2). Common Core Controversy – What does it Really Mean to Texas? Retrieved October 25, 2015, from http://educatefortexas.com/commoncoretexas/

Levine, M., & Levine, A. (2013). Holding accountability accountable: A cost–benefit analysis of achievement test scores. *American Journal of Orthopsychiatry, Vol. 83*(Issue 1), 17-26.

Rafool, B., Sullivan, E., & Al-Bataineh, A. (2012). Integrating Technology Into The Classroom. Retrieved November 15, 2015, from http://eds.b.escohost.com/eds/pdfviewer/pdfviewer?sid=2c9f1dc1-4c58-41dd-a242-210e6e014d4e@sessionmgr113&vid=13&hid=108

Starr, J., & Spellings, M. (2014). Examining High-Stakes Testing. *Academic Journal, Vol. 14*(Issue 1), P70-77, 8p.

Vega, V. (2013, February 5). Technology Integration Research Review. Retrieved November 15, 2015, from http://www.edutopia.org/technology-integration-research-learning-outcomes

http://www2.ed.gov/policy/eseaflex/secretary-letters/wad6.html

https://tslpresource.org/lasers/texas-state-literacy-plan-overview

http://www.iste.org/standards/iste-standards/standards-for-teachers

http://www.dallasisd.org/cms/lib/TX01001475/Centricity/domain/98/evaluation/11-12/finalrpts/EA11-301-2-SCE-Report-Final.pdf

Article 12

Accountability Should Be The Measuring Stick In Education Presentation

With the passage of "Every Student Succeeds Act," key players in education are celebrating the victory of eliminating the No Child Left Behind Law. The battle has been won but the war is still intense when it comes to the academic success of our nation's kids. Teacher accountability still needs to be looked at when it comes to educating students. The blame has too often been placed on high stakes testing or students who teachers feel are unteachable. Now that high stakes testing has been eliminated teachers will no longer have an excuse or anyone to blame. They will have to present their A-Game when it comes to meeting or exceeding the expectations of their state education agencies.

Recommendations for Dallas ISD

There are 5 key highlights in "Accountability Should Be The Measuring Stick In Education." These highlights are recommendations for Dallas ISD. They include teacher accountability, taking another look at the No Child Left Behind Law, the Every Student Succeeds Act, assessments and incorporating technology in the classroom.

Teacher accountability should be top priority because our students' academic success is tied to great educators. They are the gateway of knowledge and information for students. Teachers hold the keys to a well rounded public school education which is the foundation for all students. Educators who inherently know this will give all students a quality education. They will also utilize differential instruction to match their classroom demographics.

The No Child Left Behind Law was not all bad. It would be in our best interest to take another look at the No Child Left Behind Law. There are some key benefits that can be incorporated when states begin to draft their own success plans for education. For example, NCLB did a good job of making data an important part of the school improvement process and of exposing the persistent achievement gaps at even the most high achieving schools. (Starr & Spellings, 2014) The No Child Left Behind Law also introduced accountability testing in our nation's schools. It was through the idea of high stakes testing that states, school districts, teachers and students were held accountable. Teachers need to be held accountable for covering all the state objectives with students to prepare them for their state exams at the end of the year. We also need to take a closer look at deficiencies at all levels in education.

The Every Student Succeeds Act ushers in more flexibility and stability after years of uncertainty about the future of No Child Left Behind. Critics said states would feel less pressure to fix the worst-performing schools. However, educators will continue to be responsible for assessing their students. States must test students yearly in reading and math in grades three through eight, and once in high school. The bill will end the federal guidelines for defining school quality and require states to set up their own accountability systems to measure improvement. States will also determine how to intervene in the bottom 5% of schools and those with low graduation rates. States must also show test data for children in different "subgroups" of students, such as racial minorities, students in poverty and English-language learners. Overall, the bill allows states to devise their own ways to address achievement gaps. (Brody, 2015)

Assessments will always be needed in our nation's schools. High stakes testing has been eliminated which makes states, school districts, teachers and students feel at ease. Now teachers can give assessments without the fear of losing federal funding for their school district. Assessments are key tools to evaluate student progress and learning. Assessments are needed and should not be eliminated. Testing received a bad reputation in the No Child Left Behind Law because loss of funding and severe consequences were embedded in the law.

Incorporating technology in the classroom will help teachers in Dallas ISD exceed the Texas Education Agency's expectations. Dallas ISD can also improve student assessment scores by implementing technology in their curriculums. With more schools statewide not meeting Annual Yearly Progress, many educators and administrators feel that students are not engaged in the curriculum and have not been motivated to learn the material they learn in the classroom. By using modern technologies that students are familiar with, teachers can integrate similar technologies and use these to their advantage as an attempt to motivate and engage learners. Starting at a young age, children are introduced to visual learning. Even babies today are subjected to technological toys such as baby mp3 players, video equipment, and computer programs developed to give them a head start on their learning. (Rafool, et al, 2012)

Educators can use software that specifically tracks the mastery of each reading objective that is outlined in the Texas Essentials Knowledge and Skills for each grade level. The suggested technology software program is a Universal Online Reading Program with an Accountability System Tracker working in concert with the Texas State Literacy Plan. Educators can also utilize release tests taken by students in the previous school years to help prepare students in the current year.

Teachers can allow students to take timed tests on the computer at school over reading objectives taught that week. Each student can work independently on their assessments and once they have mastered an objective they can advance to the next. Computerized tests are benefitual for both students and teachers because students don't have to wait for their results and teachers can give immediate feedback. Effective teachers model and apply the ISTE Standards for students as they design implement, and assess learning experiences to engage students and improve learning; enrich professional practice; and provide positive models for students, colleagues, and the community. All teachers should meet the following standards and performance indicators. (http://www.iste.org/standards/iste-standards/standards-for-teachers)

Three Methods To Improve Dallas ISD Test Scores

An action plan for Dallas ISD include creating a solid state curriculum and testing tool, which Texas has already created. Texas has an educational plan for every core subject called the Texas Essentials Knowledge and Skills (TEKS) which is the state curriculum. These skills are tested with the state mandated testing tool called the State of Texas Assessments of Academic Readiness (STAAR). Dallas ISD has identified its At-Risk Students so educators can draft curriculums to meet the needs of those students. Texas has also drafted its plan to detail what should be included in a state mandated curriculum to make sure students are college ready. The plan has been drafted and educators need to become more efficient and strategic at working the plan.

Texas also has the Texas State Literacy Plan implemented in school districts. The plan is used to accomplish academic success in reading for K to 12 grade levels. It also includes valid and reliable assessments, including the use of assessments that are appropriate for English language learners which are used to gather information. Data analysis informs all levels of decision making, systematic, explicit, and coherent instruction utilizing evidence-based instructional materials and practices in reading and writing is provided following the Texas Essential Knowledge and Skills in English and Spanish, the English Language Proficiency Standards across all grade levels and content areas, and the College and Career Readiness Standards for every school-age student. Effective instruction, differentiated based on assessed needs, is provided to all learners through a response to intervention framework. Classroom teachers, interventionists, and specialists in dyslexia, gifted and talented education, special education, and bilingual and English as a second language programs coordinate to meet the diverse needs of all learners, achievement goals are clearly defined, and progress is monitored at every age and grade level. (https://tslpresource.org/lasers/texas-state-literacy-plan-overview)

Teacher Accountability should also be a top priority in Dallas ISD. It includes documentation of standards taught and differential instruction to match class demographics. Teacher accountability for student assessments should be monitored throughout the year. Waiting for test results at the end of the year is too late to turn things around for teachers and students. In order for success to come from any educational policy or law accountability must be demanded in the assessement process throughout the year. Teachers should be required to show documented evidence that objectives were covered and students were tested for mastery. The graded test papers are documented evidence to show student progress. It helps teachers and students by giving a preview of how students will do at the end of the year on state mandated tests. Assessments over state objectives throughout the year keeps teachers and students accountable.

What I learned During This Course

During the course of working on my project and taking this course, I learned several things about educational assessments. One key topic of interest was creating assessments that are free from biases. Tests results can be unfair when different groups are tested with assessments filled with biases. Bias means unfair or unjust. An assessment would be biased if its tasks perpetuated undesirable role stereotypes, race stereotypes, or gender stereotypes. This judgment about the offensive nature of assessment content can be called facial bias. Most large-scale tests use a panel of judges to screen test items for offensive or stereotypical material. The goal is not to produce faceless, gender-free, ethnic-free assessment materials. Rather, it is to represent gender and ethnic groups in a balanced, inoffensive, and fair way in those materials. A fair assessment or test is one that provides scores that (a) are interpreted and used appropriately for specific purposes, (b) do not have negative or adverse consequences as a result of the way they are interpreted or used, and (c) promote appropriate values. (Nitko & Brookhart, 2011)

My Perspective About Using Technology In The Classroom

While finalizing assignment 3 it affirmed my belief that effective teachers model and apply the ISTE Standards for students as they design implement, and assess learning experiences to engage students and improve learning; enrich professional practice; and provide positive models for students, colleagues, and the community. All teachers should meet the following standards and performance indicators. (http://www.iste.org/standards/iste-standards/standards-for-teachers)

Educators can utilize release tests taken by students in the previous school years to help prepare students in the current year. Teachers can allow students to take timed tests on the computer at school over reading objectives taught that week. Each student can work independently on their assessments and once they have mastered an objective they can advance to the next. Computerized tests are benefitual for both students and teachers because students don't have to wait for their results and teachers can give immediate feedback.

Educators can also utilize technology by creating an intranet website for students. The intranet website will be for an educator's core subject and for each class the educator teaches. The intranet website will allow students to create their own user names and passwords for the site. Educators can put links to different websites that can help students at home and at school. Students can review and practice lessons taught in class, play educational games, and research additional information on current and future class objectives.

Recommending Technology Tools District-Wide

Before I recommend any new technology tool school or district wide, I would first implement it in my own classroom. I am a firm believer of testing out tools, methods or curriculums first with my students. The technology tools should be tested atleast for a month to see how students respond to them. Educators should also record assessment data before and after using new technology tools. They should look for any improvements in assessment results while using the new technology. The teacher's recorded data helps give documented proof of any recommended technology tool that should be used school or district wide.

Two new technology innovations that would be practical for Dallas ISD are the Flipped Classroom concept and for special needs students the district should implement Thunder Screen Reader. Flipped Classroom would work well to help teachers maximize on time contraints.

Teachers often complain about instructional time to cover curriculum objectives with students. Lectures are normally conducted as whole group discussions. The teacher also uses this time to answer questions about the lesson that students did not understand. Teachers also limit the questions students ask because they have to cover a large amount of content. The Flipped Classroom will allow students and teachers to get the most out of classroom time. Teachers will have more time to work one on one with students as well as in groups.

Dallas ISD teachers would also benefit by incorporating the Thunder Screen Reader for their special needs students. Thunder Screen Reader is a reliable new software tool that makes computers speak. Without seeing the screen, students will be able to write letters and documents, hear what they typed letter by letter or word by word, change the speed and voice, and repeat what they have just heard and more. Thunder will speak Windows menus and dialog boxes, allowing full control of the computer. It gives full speech feedback for most text-based word processing tasks including editing documents in Microsoft Word, WordPad or Notepad. Thunder enables the blind user to keep in touch with friends and family in complete privacy by using Thunder with the popular Outlook express e-mail package. Thunder helps students create letters using Microsoft Word and provides access to the spell check function. It also works with the Microsoft Excel spreadsheet, Windows Calculator, Messenger and more. http://www.hearmore.com/store/prodView.asp?idproduct=6597&categoryi=Computer_Software

When all key players in U.S. Education take responsibility for their role in educating students there will be change and progress. Congress is responsible for passing education laws that promote academic excellence and are practical for all involved. State Education Agencies are responsible for drafting state curriculums that align with the current education law. School districts are then responsible for implementing the curriculum. Teachers must also create lesson plans that align with state mandated curriculums and students must show mastery of the objectives in each tested core subject for their grade level. When everyone is held accountable for their part in education, pointing fingers and placing blame elsewhere will be a thing of the past.

References

Brody, L. (2015, November 30). 'No Child Left Behind' Replacement Plan Shifts Power to States on Education. Retrieved December 5, 2015, from http://www.wsj.com/articles/no-child-left-behind-replacement-plan-shifts-power-to-states-on-education-1448928806

Nitko, A., & Brookhart, S. (2011). *Educational Assessment of Students* (6th ed.). Upper Saddle River, New Jersey: Pearson Education.

Rafool, B., Sullivan, E., & Al-Bataineh, A. (2012). Integrating Technology Into The Classroom. Retrieved November 15, 2015, from http://eds.b.escohost.com/eds/pdfviewer/pdfviewer?sid=2c9f1dc1-4c58-41dd-a242-210e6e014d4e@sessionmgr113&vid=13&hid=108

Starr, J., & Spellings, M. (2014). Examining High-Stakes Testing. *Academic Journal, Vol. 14*(Issue 1), P70-77, 8p.

https://tslpresource.org/lasers/texas-state-literacy-plan-overview

http://www.iste.org/standards/iste-standards/standards-for-teachers

http://www.hearmore.com/store/prodView.asp?idproduct=6597&category i=Computer_Software

Accountability Should Be The Measuring Stick In Education Presentation

https://www.youtube.com/watch?v=IaKgsc2nthA

Article 13

My Philosophy of Education Has Been Enhanced But Not Changed

As I reflect on my philosophy of education and theme for my portfolio, I notice both are similar in some areas. The classes in my Master's of Education program with a focus on Curriculum, Instruction and Assessment have enhanced without changing the overall essence of my philosophy of education. Classes such as EDU 512 Diversity in K-12 Education, EDU 510 Educational Assessments, and EDU 573 Instructional Methods have provided information and tools that work in concert with my philosophy. My philosophy of education has always included diversity. It is my passion to educate students of all races, cultures, ethnicities and all walks of life. Students should receive an equal education free of biases to be successful academically. In my philosophy of education key principles are emphasized which include education is necessary, it does not discriminate, it comes from many sources, education is continuous, it opens doors of opportunities, and accountability is the measuring stick in education.

My philosophy of education is also applied in classroom instruction. It is my belief that teachers set the standards for students. They are responsible for what happens in the classroom. Teachers must model what students are required to learn. They must reteach when necessary. Teachers and students are required to respect and practice diversity. Teachable moments are important. They provide opportunities of improvement and new information. Teachers and students are required to respect the property of others. Teachers must model acceptable behavior in the classroom. Consequences must follow an infraction. Teachers and parents must form positive alliances and communication is mandatory for all issues.

Students must also follow rules, policies and procedures. They must learn what is required for standardized tests. Students are required to give their best everyday. They must exhibit acceptable behavior and acceptable speech. Courtesy to others is mandatory. There is zero tolerance for bullying. Assignments must be the original work of students and failure is not an option.

The guiding theme for my portfolio is "Diversity in Instructional Methods and Assessments." My theme is important in education for teachers and students. Teachers are more than ever faced with teaching students who represent a global society. Students in the classroom are from all races, cultures, ethnicities and all walks of life. It is also important that teachers' instructional methods and assessments match the demographics in their classrooms. The artifacts that support my theme "Diversity in Instructional Methods and Assessments" include a video titled "Brenda Johnson's Philosophy of Education" and three written papers with picture presentations titled "A Diversified ToolBOX," "Effective & Appropriate Teaching Strategies," and "Room For Improvement In Assessment Planning."

In the video "Brenda Johnson's Philosophy of Education," it presents my life mission statement as the foundation of my beliefs as an educator. I believe in diversity. I apply it to my students in my teaching methods and assessments. In the written paper and picture presentation titled "A Diversified ToolBOX" it emphasizes that teachers must have a variety of resources to use in their toolbox. These resources must represent the demographics of teachers' classrooms. They include books, written teaching material, teaching strategies, and a multicultural curriculum.

Next, the written paper and picture presentation titled "Effective & Appropriate Teaching Strategies" emphasizes differential instruction, grouping, pre-assessments and rigor to help students. Differential instruction is important to reach all students with different learning styles. Finally, the written paper and picture presentation titled "Room For Improvement In Assessment Planning" emphasizes state mandated objectives incorporated into lesson plans, assessing special needs students, accommodations and Blooms Taxonomy trigger questions to prepare students for state tests. Students should be tested fairly with unbiased assessments. Overall, the theme for my portfolio and my philosophy of education emphasize similar principles. These principles are incorporated in my academic and personal life. These principles include diversity in resources, teaching strategies and assessments which are used to reach all students.

References

Video: Brenda Johnson's Philosophy of Education

Papers by Brenda Johnson:
A Diversified ToolBOX
Effective & Appropriate Teaching Strategies
Room For Improvement In Assessment Planning

https://strayer.optimalresume.com/previewDoc.php?tkn=235472a2b47d45130c21e9a15106c8ee-p1028789

Article 14

Embracing Research Methods

Becoming a life long learner involves educating yourself formally and informally. When teachers choose to continue their education it benefits their students. It also keeps teachers updated in their field of study. Educators should never stop improving their methods or strategies in the classroom. In order to provide "Diversity In Instructional Methods and Assessments," educators must research the best practices. The skill that is most beneficial to me is knowing how to research and the types of research such as quantitative, qualitative and mixed methods.

Quantitative research methods are expressed in the forms of variables, while the concepts in qualitative research methods are expressed in motives and generalizations. They are usually universal, like formulas for finding mean, median and mode for a set of data, whereas, in qualitative research each research is approached individually, and individual measures are developed to interpret the primary data taking into account the unique characteristics of the research. They appear in the forms of numbers and specific measurements and in qualitative research data can be in forms of words, images, transcripts, etc. Finally, research findings in quantitative research can be illustrated in the forms of tables, graphs and pie-charts, whereas, research findings in qualitative studies is usually presented in analysis by only using words. Qualitative research methods are interpretative and aim to provide a depth of understanding. Qualitative methods are based on words, perceptions, feelings etc. rather than numbers and they include experiments, interviews, focus groups, and questionnaires with open-ended questions. Mixed research involves using a combination of both methods.

(http://research-methodology.net/research-methods/qualitative-research) (http://research-methodology.net/research-methods)

Knowing how to research will lead teachers to the right sources for data. When educators conduct their own study, they should decide which data gathering tools to use such as surveys, interviews, control groups, existing data, etc. When educators know the correct data gathering tool to use, they can get the results they are seeking. Depending on the study, sometimes a sample will give data that represents a larger population. According to J. W. Creswell in *"Research Design: Qualitative, Quantitative, and Mixed Methods Approaches"* A survey design provides a quantitative or numeric description of trends, attitudes, or opinions of a population by studying a sample of that population. From sample results, the researcher generalizes or draws inferences to the population. In an experiment, investigators may also identify a sample and generalize to a population; however, the basic intent of an experimental design is to test the impact of a treatment (or an intervention) on an outcome, controlling for all other factors that might influence that outcome. As one form of control, researchers randomly assign individuals to groups. When one group receives a treatment and the other group does not, the experimenter can isolate whether it is the treatment and no other factors that influence the outcome.

Asking the right interview questions is very important to obtain key data that will help prove findings in your study. It is also up to the person doing the research to ask the right probing questions to get further details. Those who are being interviewed should understand the questions they are being asked. When participants understand the questions, they can give accurate and complete answers. It is also a good idea to give your participants a brief introduction to what your study is about and what information you seek to obtain. When participants are not interested, lack knowledge, or cannot add to your study it is a good sign they should not be used in your research.

In my study titled "Can College Students Of All Races, Cultures, Backgrounds, And Various Demographics Working Together On Projects In College Help Decrease Racism On A Bigger Scale?," I show that college students of various demographics can work together which decreases racism on a bigger scale. My study includes an example that shows students of various demographics working together to help eliminate sweatshops. The students are engaged in a common cause and race is not a factor when trying to accomplish a goal. I also include information from a study that shows how race is a factor in choosing the right college. Another study also gives findings of a survey about college students attitudes and beliefs about race. In the survey I conducted, I asked four questions which also include probing questions. The four questions include, As a hiring manager do you feel comfortable hiring a team who are apart of your race or do you prefer a team of diversity? What does diversity mean to you? If you were paid to do a book project would the person's race who hired you determine the quality of work you give back? and As a college student do you prefer to be taught by an instructor who shares your same race or any instructor of a different race who is qualified to teach the course? These questions gave feedback data that was used to support my study.

The key aspect that contributed to my interest and development in research methods was the course I took called Educational Research Methods. I am also interested in research methods because I am an author who do a lot of research for book projects. In this course I was taught how to do three types of research such as quantitative, qualitative, and mixed methods. These methods were also used in a study that each student had to complete. The name of my study was titled "Can College Students Of All Races, Cultures, Backgrounds, And Various Demographics

Working Together On Projects In College Help Decrease Racism On A Bigger Scale?" In my

study I used both qualitative and quantitative methods. Although the issue of racism is being

tackled on a college level, teachers in public schools are also dealing with the issue. Teachers

have tried many approaches to implementing Multicultural Education in the classroom.

Teachers are faced with the challenge everyday to give students a quality education meaningful

to their individual culture.

Teachers who use the Multicultural Social Justice Approach are helping students on many

levels such as democracy, analyzing institutional inequality, social action, and bridging the gap

to work with other oppressed groups. Although the Multicultural Social Justice Approach

strategically hits the target in many areas of multicultural education, the Single Group Approach

focuses on one specific group at a time so the history, perspectives, and worldview of that group

can be developed coherently rather than piecemeal. It also examines the current social status of

the group and actions taken historically as well as contemporarily to further the group's interests.

(Banks 2013, p. 48)

The Single Group approach is similar to the Multicultural Social Justice Approach. Both

approaches seek political and social change. The Multicultural Social Justice Approach deals

with political and social change no matter where it is found. The Single Group Approach deals

with political and social change as it pertains to uplifting the status of one particular group.

(Banks, 2013, p. 48)

When the Multicultural Social Justice Approach is taken, students will learn how to put democracy in action for themselves. This approach seeks to give students real life experiences of the world. The teacher's goal is to prepare students with the tools to make an impact and difference nation and world-wide. Students are given tools to recognize inequalities and tools to change those injustices. Teachers allow students to practice democracy when students vote for student council representatives, class president and the things students care deeply about. Reading the U.S. Constitution and hearing lectures on the three branches of government is a passive way to learn about democracy. For students to understand democracy, they must live it. They must practice politics, debate, social action, and the use of power (Osler & Starkey, 2005).

The Multicultural Social Justice Approach is rooted in social reconstructionism, which seeks to reconstruct society toward greater equity in race, class, gender, and disability. This approach also questions ethics and power relations embedded in the new global economy. It draws on the penetrating vision of George Bernard Shaw (1921/2004), who exclaimed, "You see things, and you say, 'Why?' But I dream things that never were, and I say, 'Why not?'" (Banks, 2013, p.50) Freire (1985) further states the Multicultural Social Justice Approach produces individuals "who organize themselves reflectively for action rather than men [and women] who are organized for passivity" (p. 82).

As an educator it is my responsibility to cover all learning styles when I create my lesson plan. Learning styles include auditory, visual and kinesthetic. My video presentation covers auditory and visual learners. Kinesthetic learners will benefit from the hands on activities given during the lecture. My video presentation also covers the Social Learning Theory by Albert Bandura. He argues that people can learn new information and behaviors by watching other people. Also known as observational learning or modeling, this type of learning can be used to explain a wide variety of behaviors. Bandura also stated that learning would be exceedingly laborious, not to mention hazardous, if people had to rely solely on the effects of their own actions to inform them what to do. Most human behavior is learned by observing and modeling from others. The observer then forms an idea about new behaviors and later uses this information as a guide for his or her actions. (Cherry, 2014)

Social Learning Theory is a combination of Situated Learning and Social Development Theory. Situated Learning is a theory by Jean Lave. He argues that learning as it normally occurs is a function of the activity, context and culture in which it is situated. Social Development Theory by Lev Vygotsky, on the other hand, states social interaction plays a fundamental role in the development of cognition. This type of learning can also challenge students' beliefs while helping to develop their critical thinking skills to solve social problems.

Finally, there are two researched based teaching techniques that I often use such as project based learning and direct instruction. Project Based Learning is a teaching method in which students gain knowledge and skills by working for an extended period of time to investigate and respond to an authentic, engaging and complex question, problem, or challenge. (http://www.bie.org/about/what_pbl)

Direct Instruction, however, is an approach to teaching. It is skills-oriented, and the teaching practices it implies are teacher-directed. It emphasizes the use of small-group, face-to-face instruction by teachers and aides using carefully articulated lessons in which cognitive skills are broken down into small units, sequenced deliberately, and taught explicitly (see Carnine, 2000, pp. 5-6; Traub, 1999). These teaching methods have worked in my classroom over the years. My students enjoy the direct instruction which gives them one on one engagement time with the teacher. The teacher sets the stage for students to receive the instruction. During direct instruction educators can also check for student mastery of the objectives in the lesson. Using project based learning gives students the opportunity to work with hands on activities. They can think for themselves and make decisions. Project based learning also allows students to plan, create and complete a project.

References

Banks, A. James. (2013). *Multicultural Education: Issues and Perspectives*. New Jersey: John Wiley & Sons, Inc.

Cherry, K. (2014, November 24). Social Learning Theory: How People Learn Through Observation. Retrieved May 12, 2017, from http://psychology.about.com/od/developmentalpsychology/a/sociallearning.htm

Creswell, J. W. (2014). *Research Design: Qualitative, Quantitative, and Mixed Methods Approaches* (4th ed.). Thousand Oaks, CA: SAGE Publications.

Excerpt from Direct Instruction Reading, by D.W. Carnine, J. Silbert, E.J. Kame'enui, S. G. Tarver, 2004 edition, p. 11.

Osler, A., & Starkey, H. (2005). *Changing citizenship: Democracy and inclusion in education*. New York: McGraw-Hill Education.

http://www.bie.org/about/what_pbl

http://research-methodology.net/research-methods/qualitative-research

http://research-methodology.net/research-methods

Article 15

Professional Development Plan

Part 1: Content Knowledge and Resources

Developing an overall effective academic and teaching plan is a challenge for many teachers.

Most teachers go into the field of Education because they have a passion to make a difference.

In order to have a lasting academic affect on students, educators must develop teaching strategies

that produce successful outcomes. These teaching strategies must be effective and appropriate

for each grade level and subject. Teachers must also develop lessons according to students'

cognitive levels. To stay abreast of the latest teaching strategies I recommend joining

professional organizations such as the International Reading Association and the National

Writing Project.

The International Reading Association (IRA) has transformed to the International Literacy

Association (ILA). It has worked to enhance literacy instruction through research and

professional development for more than 60 years. The IRA hones the skills of thousands of

literacy educators through practical research journals, publications, professional development,

conferences, and advocacy efforts. Over 900 books have been published about literacy

education through the ILA. This organization has also developed and managed dozens of global

literacy projects across the developing world. It has also built a community of educators through

a network of councils and affiliate groups. The organization also advocates before legislative

and regulatory bodies for resources to enhance students' skills. They also set standards for

educators and assessments that are now used throughout the education field. Finally, the organization co-produced ReadWriteThink, which is a website resource for peer-reviewed lesson plans. (https://www.literacyworldwide.org/about-us/our-story)

The next professional organization is the National Writing Project. The NWP is a network of sites anchored at colleges and universities and serving teachers across disciplines and at all levels, early childhood through university. They develop resources, provide professional development, generate research, and act on knowledge to improve the teaching of writing and learning in schools and communities. The National Writing Project believes that access to high-quality educational experiences is a basic right of all learners and a cornerstone of equity. They work in partnership with institutions, organizations, and communities to develop and sustain leadership for educational improvement. Throughout their work, they value and seek diversity in their organization as well as for their students and communities. They also recognize that practice is strengthened when they incorporate multiple ways of knowing informed by culture and experience. (https://www.nwp.org/cs/public/print/doc/about.csp)

In the education field I predict three issues that will remain with us for the next decade which include multiculturalism in the classroom, racism, and teacher accountability. Developing a multicultural curriculum for classroom instruction is essential because immigration continues to be the issue in our United States public school systems. Immigrants give rise to the largest part of linguistic diversity among students and are also the fastest-growing group of students in U.S. schools (Oh & Cooc, 2011). In fact, almost all the growth in the child population of the United States in the last two decades can be accounted for by children of immigrants (Cervantes & Hernandez, 2011; Fortuny, Hernandez, & Chaudry, 2010). Many demographers predict that by 2025, approximately 20 to 25 percent of immigrant students enrolled in public schools will have limited proficiency in English (Spellings, 2005).

Next, racism in the United States is outdated and should have died already. Some people are still in denial when it comes to racism in the United States. Racism is at its all time high in our society today. It is a degenerating disease that is seen as a public health hazard. Many can clearly see its affects, while others refuse to acknowledge that racism still exists. This country has a long history of mistreating humans based on race and skin color. For 400 years the United States engaged in the practice of slavery. Forced slave labor was used to build everything in this country from the ground up. This degrading practice of slavery was challenged on many occasions by the slaves and abolitionists. It wasn't until 1863, when President Abraham Lincoln signed the Emancipation Proclamation, that slaves were set free and slavery was abolished. Unfortunately, the affects of a slave system still has a major impact on how our country operates, moves and exists on a daily basis. This affect, rooted in old systems, must continue to be challenged to abolish laws that originated from the era of slavery. As a country we cannot move forward with the true essence of diversity if we are still operating under the control of a racist system.

The last issue I believe will be with us for another decade is teacher accountability. Educators are responsible for the content they share with students. The lecture content should be well put together so students can master the objectives. States are required to put in place teacher and principal evaluation and support systems that take into account information on student learning growth based on high-quality college and career-ready

(CCR) State assessments as a significant factor in determining teacher and principal performance levels, along with other measures of professional practice such as classroom observations. These systems also require that all teachers and principals receive robust, timely, and meaningful feedback on their performance and support in order to inform and improve instruction so that all students meet the expectations of new CCR standards. Including student learning growth as a significant factor among the multiple measures used to determine performance levels is important as an objective measure to differentiate among teachers and principals who have made significantly different contributions to student learning growth and closing achievement gaps. (http://www2.ed.gov/policy/eseaflex/secretary-letters/wad6.html)

Multiculturalism is a subject that educators need to fully understand. Educators can read books and articles on multiculturalism in the classroom. These resources will help teachers understand what multicultural lesson content includes and teaching strategies. The list of books and websites that should be used to understand multiculturalism in the classroom include:

Bishop, Rudine Sims. *Free Within Ourselves: The Development of African American Children's Literature.* Heinemann, 2007.

Brooks, Wanda M. and Jona C. McNair, eds. *Embracing, Evaluating and Examining African American Children's & Young Adult LIterature.* Scarecrow Press, 2008.

Fox, Dana L. and Kathy G. Short, editors. *Stories Matter: The Complexity of Cultural Authenticity in Children's Literature.* National Council of Teachers of English (NCTE), 2003

Harris, Violet H., editor. *Teaching Multicultural Literature in Grades K-8.* Christopher-Gordon, 1992.

Harris, Violet H., editor. *Using Multiethnic LIterature in the K-8 Classroom.*

Christopher-Gordon, 1997. Articles that can be read are also listed for more

information such as:

Higgins, Jennifer Johnson. <u>"Multicultural Children's Literature:Creating and Applying</u>

<u>an Evaluation Tool in Response to the Needs of Urban Educators."</u> *New Horizons for*

Learning 2002.

Caldwell, Naomi, Gabriella Kaye and Lisa Mitten. <u>"I is for Inclusion: The Portrayal of Native</u>
<u>Americans in Books for Young People."</u> Program for the ALA/OLOS <u>Subcommittee</u> for Library
Services to <u>American Indian</u> People, American Indian Library Association, June 2007.

Hill, Rebecca. <u>"The Color of Authenticity in Multicultural Literature."</u> VOYA (December 2011):
445-447.

Horning, Kathleen T. "An Interview with Rudine Sims Bishop." *Horn Book Magazine* v. 84 n. 3
(May/June 2008): 247-259.

Perkins, Mitali. <u>"Straight Talk on Race: Challenging the Stereotypes in Kids' Books."</u> *School*
Library Journal v. 55 n. 4 (April 2009): 28-31.

Part 2: Competencies

The development of information literacy throughout my master's of education degree has

improved with the topics that I researched. The different topics I read over the course of my

studies have helped me obtain more knowledge. I have learned about multiculturalism in the

classroom and what it means. I also learned about gender and racial biases on assessments.

Finally, I learned how to create assessments that are gender neutral and free from personal

biases. My three goals to develop my literacy skills are to read various pieces of information

from many sources, research topics of interest and write to discuss what I have learned. The potential means to accomplish my literacy goals include subscribing to magazines that focus on education, reading books that are topic specific for the course I teach, and joining a professional organization where I can collaborate with other professionals in education to increase my literacy in the field of education.

The strategies I plan to use to apply my literacy skills include reading to students, creating lecture content that covers all learning styles and creating assessments that are unbiased. These strategies can also be applied with direct and indirect instruction. The direct instruction strategies used in my "Writing for the Media" unit were content presentation of the subject, modeling the concepts of creating a newspaper, going over the rubric instructions for the assignment, and supplying a list of suggested tools and resources to create a newspaper. Direct instruction has certain characteristics such as an academic focus; a teacher-directed curriculum; clarity to goals; review of past learning; presentation of new material in small steps; the monitoring of student progress through questioning; provision for feedback with corrections; provision for independent exercise; and the revision of the lesson's goals based on review. Elements of direct instruction are also incorporated within software that is used to enhance the learning of at-risk students. (Smith, 2016)

The indirect instruction strategies used in my class, "The Newspaper Writer," included student hands on activities to create unique and original newspapers. Students also did interviews to get content for their newspapers, they selected the software or newspaper template to input their content, they chose photos to download or took original pictures to use with their newspaper content. Students were also given the option of having an online newspaper or printing a hard copy. Students had the task of finding ways to advertise their newspaper and get

subscribers. Newspaper feedback came from fellow classmates or peers.

My writing skills continue to improve throughout my master's of education degree program.

Opportunities to write include papers and discussion posts to demonstrate my understanding and

mastery of the course material. My writing has also improved while using information from

research on websites and books. My writing skills are also used to help fellow classmates with

critical thinking to challenge them on their research. My writing has also given me an

opportunity to use new words from content I read in books, magazines and on the internet. My

writing continues to improve as I practice collaborating with my own students, my instructor and

fellow classmates. My writing skills can be seen in artifacts I have chosen such as

"Accountability Should Be The Measuring Stick In Education," "A Diversified ToolBOX," and

"Writing For The Media: The Newspaper Writer."

My action plan to build upon my personal and professional strengths is to reading books,

magazines, newspapers and other reading material everyday to obtain information for future

writing assignments. I also write articles once a week to practice my writing skills. Lastly, I do

research on topics that interest me every month. The steps I will take to accomplish my personal

and professional goals is to set a schedule for reading books, magazines, newspapers, etc, get

feedback from friends on articles I write and create surveys for participants to help with my

research topics of interest. The means I will use to accomplish my goals are blog sites will help

with writing articles, writing organizations will help to improve writing skills, and professional

organizations will help with feedback on research topics.

Relevant strategies are my writing ability to write books, articles, classes, curriculums and lesson plans that help both children and adults. My strength in writing was used often when I wrote curriculums and lesson plans for the subject and grade level I was assigned. I have been blessed to teach Pre-Kindergarten, 3rd to 6th grade Intro to Media, 4th grade Social Studies & Science, and students enrolled in my educational program, "The Young Scholar's Book Club." When writing curriculums and lesson plans teachers have to be mindful of the grade level and demographics of their classroom. This will also determine what lesson activities to use and not use with students. Some activities are appropriate for certain grade levels and others are not. I also consider the amount of time an activity will take for students to complete. When writing curriculums and lesson plans, the objectives from the state curriculum must also be incorporated. State objectives must be incorporated because students will be tested at the end of the school year.

Part 3: Reflective Activities

The reflection goals that I set during week 3 have been accomplished. The schedule of 4:30 am at the beginning of each week moving forward was productive. I used Sunday which is the start of the week as the day to reflect on different units of the course I taught called "Intro to Media." The reflection gave me an opportunity to look at the course as a whole. I then looked at each unit in the course. Things such as field trips, hands on activities, writing skills, lecture content, multiculturalism and assessments were all reviewed in this course. On some units little improvements were needed more than others. The reflective process caused me to become a more reflective practitioner because I was forced to look at the entire course "Intro To Media." I also broke down each unit to see if improvements were needed in the lecture content, activities and assessments. This process helped me to come up with alternative activities and lecture content to help students master writing objectives for their end of the year state test.

Two ways that I would strengthen my reflective process is through journal writing and discussions with colleagues. Journal writing could mean taking notes on things I need to improve or incorporate in the next lesson. What went well or wrong in the lesson. Atleast 1 hour is good to reflect my workday and the lessons presented for the day. The place I like for reflection has to be quiet. The library, a quiet place in my home or a quiet spot at a restaurant that has WiFi. I like to reflect and I love the reflective process. It allows anyone to evaluate themselves and hold themselves accountable for their intended outcome of a lesson. Reflections consist of three vital components: (1) description, (2) analysis, and (3) future impact.

The description should emphasize the following: who, what, when, where, and how. The description component provides the foundation for the rest of the reflection. This is an important segment for the audience of the portfolio. If a clear description is provided, the other two components will be easier to write. For a beginning teacher, being able to describe the segments of an executed lesson will allow him or her to think about the process of teaching. For many beginning teachers, lessons are a whirlwind experience where they are trying to teach while managing student behavior and procedures, presenting new content, and using new methods while motivating students and remaining enthusiastic. The process of formal reflection allows these educators a chance to break down their lessons into sections, beginning by describing the process of the lesson. The best way to write good reflections is to begin by looking at models of good and bad reflections and analyzing them in terms of strengths and weaknesses. Future impact is taking the analysis and writing down improvements. These improvements could include better strategies to deliver the content in each unit. Future impact could also include alternative hands on activities to help students master objectives in the lessons. (Ghaye, 2011)

Two ways I will continue to apply reflective activities is through journaling and content analysis and review. As I reflect I write things down that I need to improve. This is a form of journaling. I reflect during the activity in case I need to redirect students back to the objective of the lesson. I also reflect at the end to see if I need to re-teach the lesson if many students did not master the objective of the lesson. My reflective goal will be in the mornings at 4:30 am while everyone in the house is asleep. I normally sit down at the kitchen table before I get my day started. I want to reflect on what I need to do for the day. I also want to reflect on the desired outcomes of the activities I planned for my students. Overall, I feel the reflection process is a great tool. I use it to hold myself and students accountable for the objectives taught in the lesson. The only weakness I want to improve in my reflection process is to think of more accommodations for my special needs students.

During reflection on content analysis and review is to make sure I have accomplished the objectives I set for my class. I also want to make sure my students have accomplished the objectives in the lesson which come from the state curriculum designed by the Texas Education Agency. I typically take an hour to reflect in the morning before my day gets started, during the execution of the lesson activity and after completing the activity. When I review the lecture content I look for ways I incorporated multiculturalism in the lesson. I also use diversity in book selections, materials, hands on activities and assessments.

References

Cervantes, W. D., & Hernandez, D. J. (2011, March). Children in immigrant families: Ensuring opportunity for every child in America. *First Focus and Foundation for Child Development.* http://www.firstfocus.net/sites/default/files/FCDimmigration.pdf.

Ghaye, T. (2011). *Teaching and learning through reflective practice: a practical guide for positive action* (2nd ed.). New York, NY: Routledge.

Oh, S. S., & Cooc, N. (2011). Immigration, youth and education: Editors' introduction. *Harvard Educational Review, 8I(3),* 396-406.

Smith, T. (2016). Direct Instruction. *Research Starters Education,* 1-1-13. Retrieved February 6, 2016.

Spellings, M. (2005). *Academic gains of English language learners prove high standards, accountability paying off* Retrieved from http://www.ed.gov/news/speeches/2005/12/l 2012005.html.

https://www.literacyworldwide.org/about-us/our-story

https://www.nwp.org/cs/public/print/doc/about.csp

http://www2.ed.gov/policy/eseaflex/secretary-letters/wad6.html

Article 16

Reflection Is Essential For Educators

Reflection is essential to designing and writing curriculums. This process allows the educator to think long term and short term about the goals of a project. Writing down the vision for a project also helps the educator visualize on paper how the project will turn out. Reflection also plays a major part in editing the content to create a multicultural curriculum. Curriculums should include all learning styles of students. When I design and write curriculums I use the reflection process while creating the curriculum, during the execution of the curriculum, and while reviewing the final outcome.

In 2009, I was invited to a college preparatory school to design and write an Elementary Media curriculum for 3rd to 6th grade. The media course gave elementary students an introduction to Newspaper, Radio, Television, Books and Magazines, and Speech & Debate. A different course unit was taught every six weeks. I embraced the reflection process to tailor the curriculum so it would fit the needs of the school. The school district never had a media curriculum for their elementary students. I wanted to make this a great experience for them.

Two objectives taught in the "Intro To Media" Radio Unit and Speech & Debate Unit include writing persuasive texts and oral & written conventions. Students write persuasive texts to influence the attitudes or actions of a specific audience on specific issues. They also are expected to write persuasive essays for appropriate audiences that establish a position and include sound reasoning, detailed and relevant evidence, and consideration of alternatives. In oral and written conventions, students understand the function of and use the conventions of academic language when speaking and writing. Students will continue to apply earlier standards learned with greater complexity. (http://ritter.tea.state.tx.us/rules/tac/chapter110/ch110b.html)

To help students master the two previous writing objectives I use direct instruction and project based learning activities. Direct instruction is used to present the lesson content for the Radio, Speeh and Debate Units. Direct instruction benefits all learners especially those who are auditory. Project based learning activities also benefits all students especially visual and kenesthetic learners. Students are required to produce written pieces for topics they choose for Radio, Speech and Debate. In the Radio Unit, students write their own commericals to educate their audience on the benefits of their products. They also write commercials to persuade audiences to purchase their product. In the Speech and Debate Unit, students write persuasive essays on controversial topics. Students are also encouraged to use visual aids such as photos, banners, posters, graphs, sound bites, music, technology and audio scripts.

During the reflection process I specified the curriculum grade levels, two example objectives used in the curriculum and the desired outcome for students. Reflection is deemed an important component of the teaching profession. The Interstate New Teacher Assessment and Support Consortium (INTASC), National Board for Professional Teaching Standards, and Pathwise (Praxis III) formalized the expectations for teaching reflection (Cady, 1998). One of the five tenets of National Board certification is the ability to reflect on practice. The tenet states, "Teachers think systematically about their practice and learn from experience." National Board–certified teachers are models of educated persons who strive to strengthen their teaching. These nationally certified teachers critically examine their practice and use this information to change or enhance it (National Board for Professional Teaching Standards, 1996) (Bullock, 2009).

My purpose to reflect is to make sure I have accomplished the objectives I set for my class. I also want to make sure my students have accomplished the objectives in the lesson which come from the state curriculum designed by the Texas Education Agency. I typically take an hour to reflect in the morning before my day gets started, during the execution of the lesson activity and after completing the activity. As I reflect I write things down that I need to improve. This is a form of journaling. I reflect during the activity in case I need to redirect students back to the objective of the lesson. I also reflect at the end to see if I need to re-teach the lesson if many students did not master the objective of the lesson. My reflective goal will be in the mornings at 4:30 am while everyone in the house is asleep. I want to spend 30 minutes to an hour journaling at the kitchen table before I get my day started. I will reflect on what I need to do for the day. I also want to reflect on the desired outcomes of the activities I planned for my students. Overall, I feel the reflection process is a great tool. I use it to hold myself and students accountable for the objectives taught in the lesson. The only weakness I want to improve in my reflection process is to think of more accommodations for my special needs students.

References

Bullock, A. A., & Hawk, P. P. (2009). *Developing A Teaching Portfolio: A Guide For Pre-Service and Practicing Teachers* (3rd ed.). Upper Saddle River, NJ: Pearson.

Cady, J. (1998). Teaching orientation: Teaching. Education, 118(3), 459–471.

National Board for Professional Teaching Standards. (1996). Middle childhood/generalist standards for National Board Certification. Detroit, MI: Author.

http://ritter.tea.state.tx.us/rules/tac/chapter110/ch110b.html

Article 17

Industry Standards In Education

After President Barack Obama passed the "Every Student Succeeds Act" in 2015 accountability measures for educators were transferred to the states. They are required to put in place teacher and principal evaluations and support systems that take into account information on student learning growth based on high-quality college and career-readiness. (CCR) State assessments are also a significant factor in determining teacher and principal performance levels, along with other measures of professional practice such as classroom observations. These systems also require that all teachers and principals receive robust, timely, and meaningful feedback on their performance and support in order to inform and improve instruction so that all students meet the expectations of new CCR standards. These objective measures are used to differentiate among teachers and principals who have made significantly different contributions to student learning growth and closing achievement gaps. (http://www2.ed.gov/policy/eseaflex/secretary-letters/wad6.html)

Industry based standards should also be used to keep educators accountable. They are the basic requirements for teachers to do their jobs. In educational settings, skill standards define a facet of student performance that is measurable and built on the skills learned as students' progress through the educational system and into the workplace. (Rahn, O'Driscoll, & Hudecki, 1999) In Industrial settings, skill standards help those involved prepare for changes in both work and the economy (Carnevale & Desrochers, 2001; Faulkner, 2002; Wills, 1995) Naquin and Wilson (2002) state that the process for establishing competency standards, assessing them, and certifying outcomes is a component of effective workforce development.

One industry based standard in education is writing curriculums. Teachers should know how to incorporate state objectives into their curriculums and lesson plans. They should also know how to develop unbiased assessments to check student mastery of objectives. When writing curriculums differential instruction should be included to meet the needs of all students. Writing curriculums will be a skill that teachers need throughout their educational careers.

In 2009, I was invited to write a curriculum titled "Intro To Media" at a college preparatory school. "Intro To Media" was a curriculum I wrote specifically for 3rd to 6th grade. Elementary students were introduced to different genres of media such as Newspaper, Radio, Television, Books & Magazines and students also learned Speech & Debate. Each semester students studied a different media genre. The artifacts titled "Writing For The Media Lesson Plan 1 Outline" and "Writing For The Media: The Newspaper Writer" are examples of the curriculum written to teach students about the Newspaper industry. The artifact titled "Media Terms & Definitions" and "Media Quiz Terms & Definitions" are also provided to show the worksheets I created for the course and what the students learned. Students also learned about the Radio and Television industry. The curriculum included field trips so students could see the inside of a Radio and Television station. They were able to connect the content they learned in class with real life radio and television experiences. Pictures are provided of me with my students at the radio and television stations we visited. The radio and television stations gave our school permission to take pictures onsite at their studios. Other artifacts provided titled "Week 3 Discussion 1 and 2" and "Week 8 Discussion 2" contain information about curriculums. The artifacts titled "Understanding Diversity Quiz" and "Understanding Diversity Quiz Answer Key" are worksheets created to get student feedback about diversity. The last artifacts provided are titled

"ASBTMSIE Presentation" and "ASBTMSIE Video" which discuss the "Every Student

Succeeds Act," curriculum and teacher accountability.

References

Carnevale, A. P., & Desrochers, D. M. (2001). Help wanted...credentails required: Community colleges in the knowledge economy. Princeton, NJ: Educational Testing Service.

Faulkner, S. (2002). National skill standards can meet local needs [Electronic version]. Learning Abstracts, 5(3), 1-2.

Naquin, S. S., & Wilson, J. (2002). Creating competency standards, assessments, and certification. Advances in Developing Human Resources, 4(2), 180-187.

Rahn, M. L., O'Driscoll, P., & Hudecki, P. (1999). Taking off!: Sharing state-level accountability strategies. Berkeley, CA: National Center for Research in Vocational Education.

Wills, J. L. (1995). Voluntary skill standards and certification: A primer. Washington, DC: Department of Education, Employment and Training Administration.

http://www2.ed.gov/policy/eseaflex/secretary-letters/wad6.html

Article 18
Performance Standards Are Important

As I reflect back over my teaching career I can see growth in my instructional methods and knowledge of the subjects I taught. As a Pre-Kindergarten teacher I was a self contained teacher who taught all core subjects to my students. Every week I created lesson plans for Math, Reading, Writing, Social Studies, Science, and Art. As I continued to progress through my teaching career, I also had the opportunity to teach 3rd to 6th grade "Intro to Media." Both opportunities have increased my knowledge and growth in 2 of the five National Board for Professional Teaching Standards propositions. These propositions include Proposition 2 which states teachers know the subjects they teach and how to teach those subjects to students and Proposition 5 which states teachers are members of learning communities.

As evidence of my growth in Proposition 2, I have provided lesson plans from my Pre-Kindergarten and Media class. These lesson plans show that I am proficient in creating and designing the curriculum and lesson plans for my students. The lesson plans also show that I have incorporated the Texas Essentials Knowledge and Skills (TEKS) state objectives in each lesson plan. The TEKS are what students must master to pass state mandated tests at the end of the year. In Texas students take the State of Texas Assessments of Academic Readiness (STAAR) test to show they have mastered the TEKS for the core subject on their grade level.

Pre-Kindergarten and Media classes are not tested over state objectives at the end of the year. However, I have always incorporated Writing and Reading TEKS in my Media classes and Pre-Kindergarten has a curriculum that is written by the state of Texas. My lesson plans follow the guidelines of the Pre-Kindergarten TEKS for all core subjects taught to my students. The TEKS listed for grades Pre-Kindergarten to 12th grades provide teachers with the objectives that must be taught in each core subject for each grade level. Teachers are held accountable for using content in their lectures, activities, classwork and homework to students master the objectives.

I have also provided written papers and class discussion from previous coursework in my Master's of Education Program. These papers and discussions are from Educational Assessment, Diversity in K to 12 Education, and Instructional Design and Development classes. The papers discuss teacher accountability, diversity, performance, and consequences. Teachers were held accountable for their students passing high stakes tests under the "No Child Left Behind" law. Although the law has been done away with, teachers are still accountable for their students passing but the stakes are not so high.

Other artifacts include a Pre-Kindergarten pre-assessment that I created and designed for my students to take at the beginning of the year. This pre-assessment gives me feedback about my students and their academic level. The scores from the pre-assessments also help me to design lesson plans and activities that meet the needs of each student. I also included from my media class student scores that were recorded on their progress reports. These three week scores are examples of what my students mastered in three week. An example of a brochure project for my fifth graders is also included as an artifact from my work environment.

As evidence of my growth with Proposition 5 which states teachers are members of learning communities, I have included minutes from the Career Day Committee meeting. I was the scribe for the Career Day Committee. I took notes when I met with other teachers to discuss the career professionals that would be invited to speak to students on career day. These minutes were recorded for the principal, teachers, and others who missed the meeting. The Career Day Committee members were responsible for contacting and scheduling business owners in the community to speak at the school. We also set up the tables, chairs, foods, beverages, and banners. We scheduled each grade level by classes to attend the event. This committee aided in my growth as a teacher because ideas were exchanges when we had our meetings. The committee also taught us how to work together to bring the community into our school. Overall, I have learned many things in my career. My strengths are in writing which aid in designing and writing curriculums. I would also like to improve in the area of quantitative and qualitative research methods.

Reflective Conversations Give Feedback

When educators enter each school year they must write and create a curriculum that will benefit all students. Teachers must incorporate all learning styles in the lesson plans. The learning styles include students who are auditory, visual and kinesthetic. Incorporating class activitites that cover all learning styles makes the lesson fun and exciting for each student. When I taught Pre-Kindergarten, a student enrolled in my class who had pre-existing problems. She was already behind in her academics because she had been taken in and out of schools. As I prepared extra lessons to get her up to grade level I discovered she had a spanish language barrier that prevented her from participating in class. My immediate course of action was to remedy the language barrier by getting suggestions from colleagues who spoke her language. The overall course of action was to send the paperwork home for her parents to sign to enroll her in a class for English Language Learners (ELL). This class will decrease the language barrier over time during the school year.

The obstacles that I faced in my course of action included books and course material written in English. My class was also taught in English without any spanish language aides. Other obstacles included the lack of student communication in English to me and fellow students. She could only immitate what she saw other students do. The language barrier was also the reason she was behind in her academics. She was not on or above grade level and special assignments had to be made to catch the student up in reading, comprehension and writing.

Opportunities include getting the student enrolled in the class for ELL students so she can work with the ESL teacher. Other opportunites include environmental print. Pictures around the room will help her understand the English language and how to read in English. Basic pictures such as traffic signs, restroom signs, pictures of items used everyday such as a cup, plate, fork, knife, spoon, etc will help my student learn vocabulary words as well.

In my master's degree program I have learned about theorists such as Lev Vygotsky, Albert Bandura, and Jean Lave. They have written theories of learning to help educators understand the development and learning process of students. Lev Vygotsky was a Russian psychologist who was born in 1896 and died in 1934. His work was largely unknown to the West until it was published in 1962. Vygotsky's theory is one of the foundations of constructivism. His theory includes three major points which are social interaction, the more knowledgeable other, and the zone of proximal development. Vygotsky believed that social interaction played a key role in the process of cognitive development. Vygotsky felt social learning precedes development. He also states "Every function in the child's cultural development appears twice. First, on the social level, and later, on the individual level. It is seen first, between people (interpsychological) and then inside the child (intrapsychological)."

Next, the More Knowledgeable Other (MKO) refers to anyone who has a better understanding or a higher ability level than the learner, with respect to a particular task, process, or concept. The MKO is normally thought of as being a teacher, coach, or older adult, but the MKO could also be peers, a younger person, or even computers.

The last point in Vygotsky's theory is the Zone of Promixal Development (ZPD) which is the distance between a student's ability to perform a task under adult guidance and/or with peer collaboration and the student's ability solving the problem independently. According to Vygotsky, learning occurred in this zone.

Vygotsky's focus was on the connections between people and the sociocultural context in which they act and interact in shared experiences. According to Vygotsky, humans use tools that develop from a culture, such as speech and writing, to mediate their social environments. Initially children develop these tools to serve solely as social functions, ways to communicate needs. Vygotsky believed that the internalization of these tools led to higher thinking skills. (https://www.learning-theories.com/vygotskys-social-learning-theory.html)

Another theorist is Albert Bandura who created the Social Learning Theory. He argues that people can learn new information and behaviors by watching other people. Also known as observational learning or modeling, this type of learning can be used to explain a wide variety of behaviors. Bandura also stated that learning would be exceedingly laborious, not to mention hazardous, if people had to rely solely on the effects of their own actions to inform them what to do. Fortunately, most human behavior is learned observationally through modeling: from observing others, one forms an idea of how new behaviors are performed, and on later occasions this coded information serves as a guide for action. (Cherry, 2014)

The last theorist is Jean Lave who created the Situated Learning theory. He argues that learning as it normally occurs is a function of the activity, context and culture in which it is situated. In contrast with most classroom learning activities that involve abstract knowledge which is and out of context, Lave argues that learning is situated; that is, as it normally occurs, learning is embedded within activity, context and culture. It is also usually unintentional rather than deliberate. Lave and Wenger call this a process of "legitimate peripheral participation." (Lave & Wenger, 1990)

Knowledge needs to be presented in authentic contexts — settings and situations that would normally involve that knowledge. Social interaction and collaboration are essential components of situated learning — learners become involved in a "community of practice" which embodies certain beliefs and behaviors to be acquired. As the beginner or novice moves from the periphery of a community to its center, he or she becomes more active and engaged within the culture and eventually assumes the role of an expert. (https://www.learning-theories.com/situated-learning-theory-lave.html)

The three artifacts I have included from my previous coursework include three written papers such as EDU 508 Assignment 2 Research Paper Part I: The Foundation, EDU 501 Assignment 2 A Radical Approach To Managing Rad's Behavior, and EDU 501 Personal Learning Theory Assignment 4. In EDU 508 Assignment 2 Research Paper Part I: The Foundation covers racism in the U. S. Racism in the United States is outdated and should have died already. With the growing rate of migrants coming from other countries, America cannot continue to live in the shadows of its racist past, old beliefs and systems. The continued mistreatment of minority groups so Caucasian Americans can feel superior should be eradicated. U. S. laws should also be updated to reflect the multicultural society that currently exists. The face of America has changed to many colors. Various races and cultures has inundated U.S. soil. Our nation must embrace change to move forward successfully in the 21st century. Extensive research has been done to understand, evaluate and change racist beliefs and behaviors beginning with college students.

The next artifact, EDU 501 Assignment 2 A Radical Approach To Managing Rad's Behavior covers understanding how to provide differential instruction, identifying At-Risk students and creating behavioral plans are among key factors in the overall academic success of students. Teachers should provide instruction that model state objectives designed by the Education Agency for their state. When educators create curriculums, they should align them with their state curriculum. The state curriculum details lesson objectives for each grade level, core subject and electives. Students will be tested for mastery of objectives for their grade level and core subject at the end of each school year. At-Risk students should be placed on an alternative plan to help them master state objectives. Students who consistently interrupt academic instruction are good candidates for behavioral plans. Teachers should provide differential instruction that matches class demographics while making sure At-Risk students get extra help from student support services.

The last artifact, EDU 501 Personal Learning Theory Assignment 4 highlights educating students should be the priority of all teachers. Students rely on professional educators to prepare them for their future. When teachers enter the field of education they should adopt the belief that all students are teachable. They must also eliminate all biases in their planned curriculum. They should also plan lesson activities for all students and their learning styles. It is important to create allies with parents. Teachers should communicate with parents about grades, student progress, and student support services. Planning for student success overall involves using a multicultural curriculum, creating lesson plans for all learning styles, and re-teaching when necessary.

Using reflective conversation for analytical thinking and problem solving is a great way to get feedback from colleagues. I used reflective conversation to get advice from colleagues who spoke both English and Spanish. During the conversation I asked questions, and my colleagues gave me suggestions of how to work with ESL students. They also gave some examples of activities that work best with ESL students. Many of my colleagues were parents. They also suggested what they did at home with their own kids who speak Spanish to improve reading, comprehension and writing skills.

Teachers who speak both English and Spanish should offer additional help to teachers who have ESL students in their classroom. The reflective conversation helps teachers open up about the problems they are having in the classroom. They also receive constructive criticism on how to turn things around. English Language Learners (ELL) in Texas school districts are considered At-Risk. These students are offered additional help to get them on track academically. The Texas State Literacy Plan is one tool I can use to help my ELL student in reading, comprehension and writing. Effective instruction, differentiated based on assessed needs, is provided to all learners through a response to intervention framework. Classroom teachers, interventionists, and specialists in dyslexia, gifted and talented education, special education, and bilingual and English as a second language programs coordinate to meet the diverse needs of all learners, achievement goals are clearly defined, and progress is monitored at every age/grade level. (https://tslpresource.org/lasers/texas-state-literacy-plan-overview)

References

Cherry, K. (2014, November 24). Social Learning Theory: How People Learn Through Observation. Retrieved April 20, 2016, from: http://psychology.about.com/od/developmentalpsychology/a/sociallearning.htm

Lave, J., & Wenger, E. (1990). Situated Learning: Legitimate Peripheral Participation. Cambridge, UK: Cambridge University Press.

https://www.learning-theories.com/vygotskys-social-learning-theory.html

https://www.learning-theories.com/situated-learning-theory-lave.html

https://tslpresource.org/lasers/texas-state-literacy-plan-overview

Article 19

Assessing My Strengths

My mission in life is to use the creative talents God gave me in writing, teaching, and speaking to not only have self-fulfillment but to also have an impact on the audience God has predestined for me. Writing, teaching and speaking are talents that have also aided in my education career. These strengths have given me overall success with my students in the classroom. I use my writing ability to write books, articles, classes, curriculums and lesson plans that help both children and adults. My strength in writing was used often when I wrote curriculums and lesson plans for the subject and grade level I was assigned. I have been blessed to teach Pre-Kindergarten, 3rd to 6th grade Intro to Media, 4th grade Social Studies & Science, and students enrolled in my educational program, "The Young Scholar's Book Club." When writing curriculums and lesson plans teachers have to be mindful of the grade level and demographics of their classroom. This will also determine what lesson activities to use and not use with students. Some activities are appropriate for certain grade levels and others are not. I also consider the amount of time an activity will take for students to complete. When writing curriculums and lesson plans, the objectives from the state curriculum must also be incorporated. State objectives must be incorporated because students will be tested at the end of the school year. My writing skills were also used when I wrote and published "The Young Scholar's Workbook: Book I Vol. I" in 2012 and "My Baby Sister" in 2013.

My speaking ability is also a strength because choosing the right words, content, and subject matter is important when delivering information to an audience. Knowing when to use the right tone, voice inflection, body language and movement is all apart of delivering a speech presentation. When I write curriculums and lesson plans I also consider the best way to deliver the lesson. I think about what words to use with my students. I make sure the vocabulary words are on or above grade level. I make sure students understand what has been said and presented to them in the lesson. There are times when students don't understand what the teacher said or what is expected in the lesson. Teachers must master giving instructions and explaining what is expected of students in classwork, homework, activities and projects.

The last strength I want to highlight is my ability to teach. The talent to teach has given me confidence as I stand in front of a classroom to present a lesson and impart knowledge to students. Teachers are expected to perform on stage everyday when presenting a lesson. They must model the objectives that students have to master in the lesson. Teaching also involves strategies used to present lesson activities. The teaching strategies I often use include Direct Instruction and Indirect Instruction.

The direct instruction strategies used in my "Writing for the Media" unit were content presentation of the subject, modeling the concepts of creating a newspaper, going over the rubric instructions for the assignment, and supplying a list of suggested tools and resources to create a newspaper. Direct instruction has certain characteristics such as an academic focus; a teacher-directed curriculum; clarity to goals; review of past learning; presentation of new material in small steps; the monitoring of student progress through questioning; provision for feedback with corrections; provision for independent exercise; and the revision of the lesson's goals based on review. Elements of direct instruction are also incorporated within software that is used to enhance the learning of at-risk students. (Smith, 2016)

At-risk children include those with special needs. Direct instruction is a great teaching tool that works in concert with small groups. Many studies suggest observational learning of academic behaviors by children with disabilities occurs during small-group direct instruction (Ledford, Lane, Elam, & Wolery, 2012). In these studies, different behaviors are taught to each group mate and, without additional teaching, participants learn both their own target behaviors and those taught to their group mates. The proposed mechanism is observational learning (Bandura, 1977): Children learn behaviors taught to others by watching those students respond correctly and be reinforced. Ledford and colleagues' 2012 review of small-group direct instruction showed that almost all children (98% of 197 participants) learned at least some behaviors taught to their peers. This finding suggests small-group instruction may be a context in which observational learning is likely. (Ledford & Wolery, 2013)

The indirect instruction strategies used in my class, "The Newspaper Writer," included student hands on activities to create unique and original newspapers. Students also did interviews to get content for their newspapers, they selected the software or newspaper template to input their content, they chose photos to download or took original pictures to use with their newspaper content. Students were also given the option of having an online newspaper or printing a hard copy. Students had the task of finding ways to advertise their newspaper and get subscribers. Newspaper feedback came from fellow classmates or peers.

Indirect instruction also has the advantage of making the student an active learner because of its constructivist nature. Learning is something that is "done by" the student, not "done to" the student, as the teacher moves from the role of instructor to one of facilitator. Indirect instruction enhances creativity and helps to develop problem-solving skills. Its resource-based nature brings depth and breadth to the learning experience. Indirect instruction means not presenting the final target concept to the learner, but allowing her/him to develop central elements independently. This involves additional steps of concept construction and also metastrategical thinking, when a choice has to be made between several alternatives with respect to a given problem. (Böttcher & Meisert, 2011)

http://spiritsd.ca/curr_content/onlineteach/instructionalstrategies/indirectinstruction/indirect.htm

The artifacts that I provided as examples of my strengths in writing are two written papers that highlight multiculturalism in the classroom. The first paper is from class EDU 512 titled "Setting the Stage for Multicultural Education in the Classroom." When teachers get to know their students at the beginning of the year they can effectively create curriculums that incorporate multicultural education. According to Banks, multicultural education has five dimensions. Establishing a multicultural education curriculum is not enough to achieve multicultural education in the classroom. He further states "Multicultural education is also a reform movement designed to bring about a transformation of the school so that students from both genders and from diverse cultural, language, and ethnic groups will have an equal chance to experience school success." The five dimensions of multicultural education are content integration, knowledge construction, equity pedagogy, prejudice reduction and empowering school culture.

The next paper is from class EDU 512 titled "Modeling Multicultural Education." In this paper, the topic of immigration is discussed. It continues to be the issue in our United States public school systems. Immigrants give rise to the largest part of linguistic diversity among students and are also the fastest-growing group of students in U.S. schools (Oh & Cooc, 2011). Other artifacts provided include 4 discussion board questions titled "Week 1 Discussion 1 EDU 533," "Week 1 Discussion 2 EDU 533," "Week 1 Discussion 2 EDU 533 pt 2," and "Week 1 Discussion 2 pt 3 EDU 533." These discussion board questions deal with a variation of multicultural curriculums and topics. The also stress the need for teachers to practice multiculturalism in the classroom to help resolve a bigger issue in society which is racism.

Multiculturalism in education will be the key to teaching students from Pre-k to 12th grade how to accept other races. It is a need that is critical and anticipated for the success of the United States. Anticipated needs are a means of identifying changes that will occur in the future. Identifying such needs should be part of any planned change so that any needed training can be designed prior to implementation of the change. On the other hand, critical incident needs are failures that are rare but have significant consequences. They are also identified by analyzing potential problems. Identifying the root causes of poor race relations in the United States is essential when implementing Multicultural curriculums in education. (Morrison et. Al, 2013)

The last two artifacts from my work environment are two published books. The first book is titled "The Young Scholar's Workbook: Book I Vol. I." This published book is a professional example of my skills in writing curriculums and lesson plans for Pre-K to 4th grade. The workbook covers all core subjects such as Language Arts, Reading, Writing, Mathematics, Social Studies and Science. The workbook also has over 100 workbook activities for Pre-K to 4th grade. The Young Scholar's Book Club offers reading enrichment, tutoring assignments, vocabulary-building skills, analytical and critical thinking skills and a whole lot more. The program provides its services via the internet, regular mail and summer workshops. The program can be accessed at www.tysbookclub.org.

My last publication is titled "My Baby Sister." It is a children's fiction book about Danielle who learns that being a big sister can be really cool. When she was 5 years old her mother announced that a baby sister or brother was on the way. Danielle's mother was pregnant with her baby sister. Danielle was excited at first until all the attention went on Kayla. As Kayla began to crawl and then walk Danielle did not like the hitting, biting and kicking that Kayla did to her. Danielle finally learned how to turn the sibling rivalry around. This children's book is also a teaching tool to help kids resolve problems as they engage with family members, friends and peers.

References

Bandura, A. (1977). Social learning theory. Englewood Cliffs, NJ: Prentice-Hall.

Banks, J. A. (Ed.). (2009). *The Routledge international companion to multicultural education*. New York and London: Routledge.

Böttcher, F., & Meisert, A. (2011). Effects of Direct and Indirect Instruction on Fostering Decision- Making Competence in Socioscientific Issues. *Res Sci Educ Research in Science Education, 43*(2), 479-506. Retrieved February 06, 2016.

Ledford, J. R., Lane, J. D., Elam, K. E., & Wolery, M. (2012). Using response prompting procedures during small group direct instruction: Outcomes and procedural variations. American Journal on Intellectual and Developmental Disabilities, 117, 413-434. http://dx.doi.org/10.1352/1944-7558-117.5.413

Ledford, J., & Wolery, M. (2013). Peer Modeling of Academic and Social Behaviors During Small- Group Direct Instruction. *Exceptional Children, 79*(4), 439-458. Retrieved February 06, 2016.

Johnson, B. (2012). The Young Scholar's Workbook: Book I Vol. I. Duncanville, TX: ASWIFTT PUBLISHING, LLC

Johnson, B. (2013). My Baby Sister. Duncanville, TX: ASWIFTT PUBLISHING, LLC

Morrison, G. R., Ross, S. M., Kalman, H. K., & Kemp, J. E. (2013). *Designing Effective Instruction* (7th ed.). Hoboken, NJ: John Wiley & Sons.

Oh, S. S., & Cooc, N. (2011). Immigration, youth and education: Editors' introduction. *Harvard Educational Review, 81(3),* 396-406.

Smith, T. (2016). Direct Instruction. *Research Starters Education,* 1-1-13. Retrieved February 6, 2016.

http://ritter.tea.state.tx.us/rules/tac/chapter110/ch110b.html

http://spiritsd.ca/curr_content/onlineteach/instructionalstrategies/indirectinstruction/indirect.htm

Article 20

Ethical Issues In Education

More and more educators are joining teacher unions and obtaining professional liability insurance to combat lawsuits. Unions fight for the rights of teachers when it comes to salaries and work related issues. When teachers obtain professional liability insurance they hope they will never use it. Teachers are sued and taken to court for many reasons by parents of children who are under the age of 18. In Texas, for example, there are many complaints filed with the Texas Education Agency against teachers and principals. Complaints include civil rights, negligence and intentional acts by educators.

Civil rights complaints allege that a public school discriminates against students on the basis of race, color, national origin, sex or disability in admission or access to, or treatment in the district's programs or activities. These complaints are under the jurisdiction and authority of the U.S. Department of Education's Office for Civil Rights (OCR). OCR and TEA enforce several federal civil rights laws that prohibit discrimination in programs or activities that receive federal funds. In addition, TEA reviews school discrimination complaints and informs individuals of the appropriate complaint resolution options.
(http://tea.texas.gov/About_TEA/Contact_Us/Complaints)

Most liability cases involve teacher negligence where teachers fail to exercise the degree of care that is necessary which results in physical injury to a student. It is important to know that teacher negligence involves four elements such as the teacher must owe a duty of care to the student, the teacher must breach that duty, the student must suffer an injury, and there must be a direct connection between the student's injury and the breach. All four elements must be in place to make a valid liability challenge by an injured student. Next, intentional acts committed against students such as assault and battery in corporal punishment cases can occur if students are punished excessively because of disruptive behavior. Slander can also occur if you leak confidential or sensitive information in one of your student's educational records to co-workers that could damage the student's standing in school or diminish the student's reputation. On the other hand, libel is when teachers write a letter of reference for a student and include negative opinions not based on facts that can prove harmful to the student. (http://www.teachhub.com/dont-get-sued-5-step-guide-teacher-liability)

When it comes to ethics in education, teachers must have a moral set of values, examine their own biases and prejudices when teaching students, and they must obey the law. Values are rules from which we make our personal decisions about what is right and what is wrong, good or bad. Values help direct us to what is more important and past what is less important. This helps guide us when making decisions. Morals tend to be broad yet are more far reaching because of their strong link to good and bad. We judge others by their morals rather than their values. Ethics, in contrast, are a set of rules that tend to be adopted and upheld by a group of people. This could include medical ethics, journalism and advertising ethics and educational ethics. So ethics or intent, tends to be viewed as something upheld and adopted internally, such as professionalism, while morals are ideals we impose on others. (Futterman, 2015)

Teachers should never incorporate their biases and prejudices in their curriculums, lesson plans or assessments. They must be fair and objective in their grading practices. One way to keep teachers accountable in their grading practices is to use rubrics for assignments they give students. The rubric is objective and it details what is expected from students in the assignment. When students grades are questioned on an assignment the rubric is used to analyze if the student completed everything in the assignment. Teachers must also practice multiculturalism in the classroom. They must recognize all distinct cultures. They must also have diversity in their curriculums and assessments. Teachers should choose books and materials for their lesson plans that match the demographics of their classroom.

Teacher Accountability should also be a top priority in all school districts. It includes documentation of standards taught and differential instruction to match class demographics. Teacher accountability for student assessments should be monitored throughout the year. Waiting for test results at the end of the year is too late to turn things around for teachers and students.   In order for success to come from any educational policy or law accountability must be demanded in the assessement process throughout the year. Teachers should be required to show documented evidence that objectives were covered and students were tested for mastery. The graded test papers are documented evidence to show student progress. It helps teachers and students by giving a preview of how students will do at the end of the year on state mandated tests. Assessments over state objectives throughout the year keeps teachers and students accountable.

The three artifacts that I provide to support this discussion include a paper titled "Accountability Should Be The Measuring Stick In Education: Assignment 2," a discussion post titled "Week 11 Discussion 1 EDU 510," and a discussion post titled "Week 7 Discussion 1 EDU 510." In the paper "Accountability Should Be The Measuring Stick In Education: Assignment 2" details the U.S. Department of Education, state agencies, school districts, administrators, teachers, students and parents alike should all have a part when it comes to accountability. When accountability breaks down at any level everyone suffers because of the weak link. It is imperative that the importance of education is upheld at all levels so the standard of excellence will not be lost.

In Week 11 Discussion 1 EDU 510, it talks about performance based tests which include speeches, presentations, group projects, independent projects, etc. When students are giving the opportunity to show what they have learned they can also be creative. Teachers have the opportunity to see what students have learned instead of getting all of their data from a pencil and paper test. Students should also be given a rubric with performance based assessments. The rubric keeps teachers and students on the same page with the same expectations. The last artifact that I provide is Week 7 Discussion 1 EDU 510 which talks about the content for assessments should not be a secret or surprise. Teachers should not hide lesson material from students that will be on their tests. This practice is unfair and unethical when it comes to grades that will be used to measure student achievement. Some teachers use this practice to fail students. A teacher's job involves helping each student reach their maximum potential of success.

References

Futterman, L. (2015, March 31). Beyond the Classroom: The importance of ethics in education. Retrieved June 2, 2017, from http://www.miamiherald.com/news/local/community/miami-dade/community-voices/article17030966.html

http://tea.texas.gov/About_TEA/Contact_Us/Complaints

http://www.teachhub.com/dont-get-sued-5-step-guide-teacher-liability

Article 21

Integrating Video To Teach How To Pass A Bill Into A Law

Presentation

In wake of the chokehold death of Eric Garner at the hands of a Staten Island, NY police officer that rendered a no indictment charge, there is now a push to reform our justice system. The urgency of reforming our justice system was also prompted by other deaths such as Michael Brown, Trayvon Martin, John Crawford III and Tamir Rice which were also at the hands of police officers and a security guard that rendered a no indictment charge or conviction. When the grand jury decided that there's no probable cause to indict Officer Daniel Pantaleo, the man who put Garner in that chokehold on a Staten Island sidewalk, it caused an outcry and mobilization of protests around the country. The New York City medical examiner's office also offered pertinent facts when it classified Garner's death as a homicide this summer. He died because of a "compression of neck (chokehold). (Botelho, 2014)

The laws that frame our justice system have been around for years. Lawmakers called for broad criminal justice reform at a hearing Tuesday in response to recent killings of black men by white police officers. Sen. Cory Booker (D-N.J.) said that though it would be prudent for the investigations of those shootings to be completed, protests over the shootings were driven by larger inequality in the prison system. (McCabe, 2014)

The federal government is now launching an investigation into the deaths of Eric Garner, Michael Brown, Trayvon Martin and others to determine if their civil rights were violated. The

Leadership Conference has already drafted a Criminal Justice Reform Initiative that deals with changing the laws to prevent police brutality on citizens. (http://www.civilrights.org/donate/resources/issues--strategies/criminal-justice-reform.html)

It is an asset for students to learn how our justice system works on a local, state and federal level. Students also need to know what takes place when a bill is introduced to congress and eventually becomes a law. Laws passed by congress become the rules and regulations that citizens live by. Laws also have specific consequences if violated.

In this presentation students will learn the specifics of how a bill becomes a law by integrating video using YouTube, Vimeo, PowerPoint and Prezi presentation tools. These presentation tools will allow students to take a peek into the congressional chambers of state representatives and senators debating whether or not certain bills should become laws. YouTube and Vimeo are technology tools integrated into the lesson to help students visualize and understand the process of how a bill becomes a law.

YouTube and Vimeo are excellent tools to show students firsthand the activities of congress. The benefits of using video in the classroom according to Ronald Berk is improved attitudes toward content and learning, it increase memory of content and understanding. He also says a video can have a strong effect on your mind and senses. It is so powerful that you may download it off the Internet or order the DVD from Amazon along with the CD soundtrack so you can relive the entire experience over and over again. This attraction to videos extends to movies, TV programs, commercials, and music videos. (Berk, 2009)

YouTube is the web's largest and most famous video sharing website and it boasts Number 3 rankings in the Alexa U.S. and World categories. Its content is user-supplied, including some serious stuff such as TED talks and the Khan Academy, along with lots of unserious stuff such as your recent vacation movies and immense numbers of cute pet videos. (O'leary, 2013)

In 2004, Vimeo was founded by a group of filmmakers who wanted to share their creative work and personal moments from their lives. As time went on, likeminded people discovered Vimeo and helped build a supportive community of individuals with a wide range of passions. Today, millions of people from all around the world enjoy Vimeo. (http://vimeo.com/about) Video footage can be used to discuss each step in the process of a bill presented on the floor of congress.

The first step in the process is when an idea needs to be developed to improve a community. Ideas are also presented in congress when a problem within a community needs to be resolved. They can come from a citizen in the community or a law maker in congress. Ideas are written up as a bills to be placed in the hopper which is a box where a proposed legislative bill is dropped and thereby officially introduced. (dictionary.com)

Video footage can be shown about project developments, ongoing problems, town hall meetings, and community leaders taking action to address the needs and problems of the people. Video footage can also be shown with the second step when the bill goes to congress. Students can witness a bill from its introduction to congress to the final step of the president signing it into law. The process will be broken down in small segment video clips to allow students to discuss, do activities, or further research on each step.

The second step in the bill process also requires Prezi and Power Point Presentations. Prezi lets users create presentations on a single, large canvas and build conceptual maps that show how ideas relate to one another. The presentations are a series of choreographed moves, zooms, and pivots across that canvas. While traditional presentations, like Power Point, proceed through a set course of slides in a linear fashion. A user viewing a Prezi-based presentation can break out of the point-by-point walkthrough at any time to get a look at the big picture, revisit an earlier subject, or take a detour into an optional area of the presentation designated by the author. (Schiller, 2011)

Prezi now has over 40 million users and it attributes its rapid growth to the increasing need for effective communication in this era of information overload. Prezi's CEO and cofounder, Peter Arvai, says, "When you deliver a presentation, you're competing against everything for your audience's attention. Prezi helps you organize your thoughts and deliver them in a clearer way that really helps your audience understand and remember your message." (Marketwired, 2014)

Prezi and Power Point are used for content related presentations that students can read. Prezi and Power Point, however do allow the author to insert video clips in Prezi and Power Point presentations. It is a great idea to use video, written content, and audio to benefit all types of learners.

The third step in the bill process is when the house committee or the senate gets the bill, studies it and then debates it. If the house gets the bill first the members of the house committee will study the bill, debate it and then vote to pass or veto it. If the bill passes it will go on to the senate floor. The senate will repeat the same steps as the house committee. When the bill is debated in the senate a filibuster or cloture can occur. When there is a filibuster a member of the legislative assembly uses irregular or obstructive tactics to prevent the adoption of a measure generally favored or to force a decision against the will of the majority by making long speeches. Cloture is a method of closing a debate and causing an immediate vote to be taken on the question. (dictionary.com)

Different versions of the bill passed through congress is made into a unified bill by a conference committee. The house and senate debate and vote on the unified bill. If the bill is approved by the house and senate it goes to the president to be signed or vetoed. If the president signs the bill it becomes a law. If the president vetoes the bill 2/3 of both houses is needed to override the veto for the bill to become a law. (www.cyberlearning-world.com/.../civics/how_a_bill_becomes_a_law.ppt)

When students witness through video the process of passing a bill into a law it helps them understand our justice system. Students are empowered with knowledge and are equipped to carry out the right actions in their communities. Students can also make a difference by initiating change in our justice system. Today's students are tomorrow's leaders. Our government provides the rules and regulations we follow daily. It is imperative that our students understand the justice system and every aspect of the three branches of government.

References

O'leary, Mick. (2013). Vimeo: YouTube's Better-Looking Little Brother. Infotoday.com.

Berk, Ronald A. (2009). Multimedia Teaching with Video Clips: TV, Movies, YouTube, and MTVU in the College Classroom. International Journal of Technology in Teaching & Learning. Vol. 5 Issue 1, p. 1-21.

Botelho, G. (2014, December 8). Was a New York Police Officer's Chokehold on Eric Garner Necessary? *CNN*. Retrieved December 14, 2014, from http://www.cnn.com/2014/12/04/us/eric-garner-chokehold-debate/index.html

McCabe, D. (2014, December 9). Lawmakers Call for Criminal Justice Reform after Brown, Garner Cases. *The Hill*. Retrieved December 14, 2014, from http://thehill.com/homenews/senate/226516-lawmakers-call-for-criminal-justice-reform-after-brown-garner-cases

Prezi Announces 40 Million Users. (2014, April 14). *Marketwire*. Retrieved December 14, 2014, from http://www.marketwire.com

Schiller, K. (2011, September 1). High- Tech Classrooms. *Sep2011, Vol. 28 Issue 8, P34-35. 2p.* Retrieved December 14, 2014, from http://www.infotoday.com

http://www.dictionary.com

http://www.vimeo.com/about

http://www.cyberlearning-world.com/.../civics/how_a_bill_becomes_a_law.ppt

http://www.civilrights.org/donate/resources/issues--strategies/criminal-justice-reform.html

About The Author

About the Author

Brenda Diann Johnson is the CEO/Founder of The Young Scholar's Book Club. The Young Scholar's Book Club is a organization that offers a free educational program for Pre-K through 4th grade. The program offers reading enrichment, tutoring assignments, vocabulary building skills, analytical and critical thinking skills and a whole lot more.

The Book Club was started with Pre-K through 4th grade in mind. Ms. Johnson's vision is to help elementary students, Pre-K through 4th grade read more, increase in their vocabulary, learn how to analyze and critique what they have read and have fun in the process of learning.

Ms. Johnson hopes to give any student around the world who joins "The Young Scholar's Book Club," encouragement, the tools to do better on assignments in school, a broader vocabulary, a love for reading and exploring new information in books.

The Young Scholar's Book Club can be accessed online at www.tysbookclub.com. The curriculum program runs from August to May each year. Students also enjoy summer workshops and seminars.

Ms. Johnson has a B. A. Degree in Broadcast Communications and a Masters of Education Degree in Curriculum, Instruction & Assessment.

Ms. Johnson is also the founder of ASWIFTT ENTERPRISES, LLC. She is an experienced educator who has taught and tutored students, Pre-K through college. Ms. Johnson is the Dean of Education, Curriculum & Instruction at Best Practices Training Institute (B.P.T. I.). She has also authored books and articles.

Ms. Johnson currently lives in Texas with her family.

Books and Services at brendadiannjohnson.com

ASWIFTT ENTERPRISES, LLC

Business advertising for Print & Media

BOOK PUBLISHING

RADIO

T.V.

Newspaper

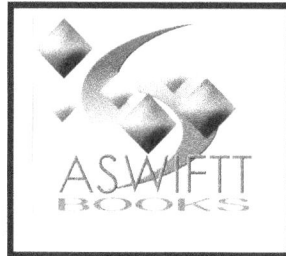

We have affordable advertising packages in our media categories. Some Ads are as low as $35.00.

You can visit us online at: www.aswifttbooks.com or e-mail us at: aswifttbookpublishing@yahoo.com

ASWIFTT BOOKS

(Ambassadors Sent With Information For This Time)

ASWIFTT ENTERPRISES, LLC creates businesses that write and publish for all three (3) media genres such at radio, tv and newspaper that focus on delivering timely, newsworthy and accurate news stories. The media genres also report on local, regional, national, and international topics.

The Young Scholar's Workbook: Book I Vol. I
(www.tysbookclub.com)

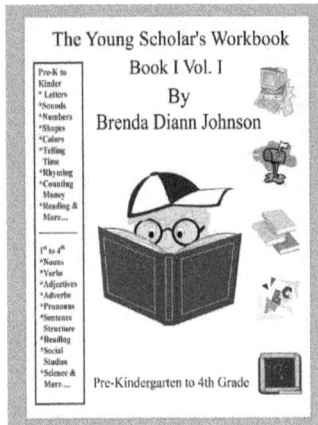

Advertise in

ASWIFTT BOOKS

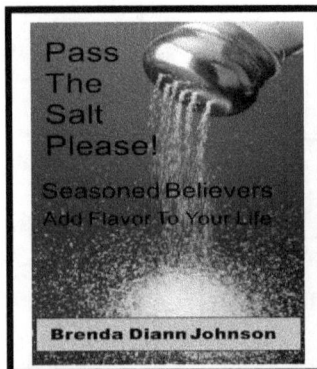

ASWIFTT ENTERPRISES, LLC ORDER FORM

Name_____

Address_____

City_____

State_____

Zip_____

Item _____Amount_____

Item _____Amount_____

Item _____Amount_____

Add $8.50 for Shipping and Handling on books

Total:_____

Make Checks, Money Orders, Cashier's Checks out to:

ASWIFTT ENTERPRISES, LLC

P.O. Box 380669

Duncanville, Texas 75138

Credit Card Orders:

Circle One: Master Card   Visa   American Express   Discover

Credit Card Number_____

Exp. Date_____

Three Digit Security Number on back of Card_____

Name & Address Associated with Credit Card:

_____

Email: _____

_____ _____

Authorization Signature   **Date**

Your order will be processed or shipped 2 to 4 weeks from the date order is received. Direct concerns on orders email: aswifttbookpublishing@yahoo.com

Thank you for your business! Make copies of this form.

www.ingramcontent.com/pod-product-compliance
Lightning Source LLC
Chambersburg PA
CBHW062041090426
42740CB00016B/2979